CENTRE FOR EUROPEAN AGRICULTURAL STUDIES

THE IMPACT OF
ENVIRONMENTAL LEGISLATION
UPON AGRICULTURE

A seminar sponsored
by the Anglo-German Foundation for the
Study of Industrial Society
held at Wye on
March 14-16 1984

Edited by:

Bernarde Duesenberg
Bridget Girling

WYE COLLEGE, ASHFORD, KENT, ENGLAND.

Seminar Papers No. 16

Copyright CEAS 1984

ISBN 0905 378 30 X

ISSN 0307 1111

Price: £ 7-00

2

ACKNOWLEDGMENTS

The outline of this seminar on the impact of environmental legislation
upon agriculture was submitted for possible sponsorship to the Board of
the Anglo-German Foundation for the Study of Industrial Society. The
Centre for European Agricultural Studies, Wye College (University of
London) acknowledges with grateful thanks the generosity of the Board in
agreeing to sponsor the seminar, together with the subsequent
publication of the papers presented. Special thanks go to
Mrs. Barbara Beck, Director of the Foundation, for sparing the time to
participate throughout the event.

BACKGROUND TO THE SEMINAR

Agriculture, which employs a minority of the population (3 per cent in UK, 6 per cent in the FRG, 8 per cent in France), is responsible for the use of the majority of the land of a nation (80 per cent in UK, 50 per cent in the FRG, 59 per cent in France). Therefore agricultural practices have a considerable impact on the quality of the environment on the one hand and the landscape of the countryside on the other.

The farmer is not only responsible for the "well-being" of soil, water and air, but also for the amenity of landscape and the abundance of flora and fauna. Traditionally it is supposed that all farming is beneficial for the environment as the farmer naturally has a vested interest in the conservation and enhancement of his basic resources. But more and more doubts are being voiced that modern agriculture, with its "farming is business" attitude, is aimed at profits for a few in the short run, to the detriment of benefits for all in the long run. Those benefits may have been experienced in terms of health and of amenity.

Environmental legislation could and should not only prevent the worst abuses, but in combination with economic measures, also encourage an improvement of the situation. It can be argued that existing legislation, however, is largely ineffective, because it is either inadequate in scope or not applied. There are significant differences between the de jure and de facto situations both within and between individual Member States, the latter leading to a distortion in the competitiveness of agricultural production according to Articles 100 and 235 of the Treaty of Rome. Such distortion suggests the need for common EC legislation to a far greater extent than has existed up till the present.

In view of this background, it was felt that it would be useful to pool experience and ideas as to how the costs and benefits of a healthier and more pleasant environment can be shared more equitably by farmers and non-farmers. The Centre for European Agricultural Studies decided to draw upon the situations in the Federal Republic of Germany and the United Kingdom as the basis for a seminar whose objective would be to provide:

1) a review of the present de jure state of environmental legislation and its application to agriculture

2) a review of the de facto effectiveness of the environmental legislation and its application

3) an economic evaluation of the effects of the de facto application of environmental legislation and of possible changes therein upon agricultural production and consumer benefits.

Ian G. Reid
Director, CEAS

THE IMPACT OF ENVIRONMENTAL LEGISLATION ON AGRICULTURE

(March 14-16, 1984)

Page

Wednesday, 14 March

SESSION I   Chairman: Mr. Ian REID (Director, CEAS)

Environmental legislation - the de jure situation

Speaker FRG: Herr W. PREUSKER (Verband Chemischer   1
   Industrie, Frankfurt-am-Main)

Speaker UK: Mr. P. CRITCHLEY (Department of the   11
   Environment, London)

Speaker on the EEC: Mr. N. HAIGH (Institute of   25
   European Environmental Policy, London)

Thursday, 15 March

SESSION II   Chairman: Dr. Bryn GREEN (Wye College)

The effectiveness of environmental legislation -
the de facto situation

Speaker UK: Mr. D. BALDOCK (Institute of European   31
   Environmental Policy, London)
Speaker FRG: Herr R. ELSNER (Bundesministerium für   34
   Ernährung, Landwirtschaft u. Forsten, Bonn)

Speaker EEC: Mr. H. DAVID (Bureau Européen de   52
   l'Environnement, Brussels)

SESSION III Chairman: Professor J.S. NIX (Wye College)
Assessing the cost of environmental legislation to
the farmer

Speaker UK: Mr. Nigel WILLIAMS (Farm Business Unit,   58
   Wye College)

Speaker FRG: Dr. E. BERG (University of Bonn)   77

(v)

Friday, 16 March

SESSION IV   Chairman: Mr. Ian G. REID (Director, CEAS)

The effects of an implementation of stricter
legislation: the reaction of the consumer

Speaker FRG: Professor W. HEESCHEN   94
    (Bundesanstalt für Milchforschung, Kiel)

Speaker UK: Emeritus Professor G.P. WIBBERLEY   111
    (Wye College)

THE IMPACT OF ENVIRONMENTAL LEGISLATION ON AGRICULTURE
(March 14 - 16, 1984)

LIST OF PARTICIPANTS

Mr D Baldock   Institute of European Environmental Policy,
                        10 Percy Street, London WC1

Mrs B Beck   Anglo-German Foundation,
                        17 Bloomsbury Square, London WC1

Dr E Berg   Institut für Landwirtschaftliche Betriebslehre,
                        Meckenheimer Allee 174, Bonn

Miss P Bury   Farm Business Unit, School of Rural Economics,
                        Wye College

Mr J Clarke   Royal Institute of Chartered Surveyors
                        (Messrs G Webb & Co), 43 Park Road, Sittingbourne,
                        Kent

Mr P Cobb   Farming and Wildlife Advisory Group,
                        c/o Wye College

Mr D Conder   Council for the Preservation of Rural England,
                        4 Hobart Place, London SW1

Dr J Conrad   International Institute for Environment and
                        Society, Potsdamerstr. 58, Berlin 30

Mr P Critchley   Department of the Environment,
                        2 Marsham Street, London SW1P 3EB

Mr T Crotty   ICI plc, Agricultural Division, PO Box 1,
                        Billingham, Cleveland TS23 1LB

Mr H David   Bureau Européen de l'Environnement,
                        Rue Vautier 29, 1040 Brussels

Miss B Duesenberg   Centre for European Agricultural Studies,
                        Wye College

Mr R Elsner   Bundesministerium für Ernährung, Landwirtschaft u.
                        Forsten, Rochusstr. 1, 53 Bonn

Dr B Green   Department of Environmental Studies and Countryside
                        Planning, Wye College

Mr N Haigh   Institute of European Environmental Policy,
                        10 Percy Street, London WC1

Prof. W Heeschen   Bundesanstalt für Milchforschung,
                        Hermann-Weigmannstr. 1, 2300 Kiel

Dr P Hinrichs	Bundesforschungsanstalt für Landwirtschaft, Bundesallee 50, 3000 Braunschweig
Mr I Hodge	Department of Land Economy, University of Cambridge, 19 Silver Street, Cambridge
Mr H Jankowski	Commission of the European Communities, DG XII, 200 Rue de la Loi, 1049 Brussels
Dr D Kurrer	Arbeitsgemeinschaft der Verbraucher e.v. (Bonn) Acacialaan 17, B-1990 Hoeilaart, Belgium
Mr P Leonard	Countryside Commission, John Dower House, Crescent Place, Cheltenham, Glos.
Mr C Major	British Agro-Chemicals Association Ltd, Alembic House, 93 Albert Embankment, London SE1
Dr S McRae	Department of Environmental Studies and Countryside Planning, Wye College
Mr M Moulton	Beechams Ltd, Beecham House, Brentford, Middlesex TW8 9BD
Prof. J S Nix	Farm Business Unit, School of Rural Economics, Wye College
Mr P Oakley	Lloyds Bank plc, Head Office, 71 Lombard Street, London EC3
Mr M Payne	National Farmers' Union, Agriculture House, Knightsbridge, London SW1
Mr O Pompl	Bayerisches Staatsministerium für Ernährung, Landwirtschaft und Forsten, Ludwigstrasse 2, D-8000 München 22
Dr A Power	Ministry of Agriculture, Fisheries and Food 55 Whitehall, London SW1A 2EY
Mr W Preusker	Verband der Chemischen Industrie, Karlstrasse 21, 6000 Frankfurt-am-Main
Mr Ian Reid	Centre for European Agricultural Studies, Wye College
Mr W de Salis	Country Landowners' Association, 16 Belgrave Square, London SW1

Mr D Skilbeck   The Ernest Cook Trust, c/o Estate Office,
                        Fairford Park, Fairford, Glos. GL7 4JH

Mrs P Teherani-   International Institute for Environment and
         Kronner   Society, Potsdamerstr. 58, Berlin 30

Prof. G P Wibberley   7 Upper Bridge Street, Wye

Mr N Williams   Farm Business Unit, School of Rural Economics,
                        Wye College

Mr M Winter   Bartlett School of Architecture and Planning,
                        University College London, Gower Street, London WC1

Mr H Zimmermann   NDS Ministerium für Ernährung, Landwirtschaft u.
                        Forsten, Calenberger Str. 2, Hannover 1

SESSION I

THE IMPACT OF ENVIRONMENTAL LEGISLATION UPON AGRICULTURE
The de jure situation in the Federal Republic of Germany

Werner Preusker
Verband Chemischer Industrie, Frankfurt

I. Legislation and Administration in the Federal Republic of Germany

The Federal Republic of Germany consists of eleven "Länder" (or
states) with their own legislation and administration. Apart from the
federal organisation, the right of local communities and districts to
self government should also be mentioned.

The power to legislate belongs to the Länder, unless the Basic
Constitutional Law (Grundgesetz) specifies that it comes under the
authority of the Federation. On certain subjects the Federation can
legislate exclusively, concurrently with the Länder or by issuing
framework laws to be completed by the Länder. Framework laws like the
Bundesnaturschutzgesetz (Federal Nature and Landscape Protection Law)
and the Wasserhaushaltsgesetz (Water Management Law) consist partly of
regulations which are binding on the whole country and partly of set
frameworks which can be and must be filled out by Länder laws.

Local communities and districts are entitled to issue their own
regulations in respect of their own affairs, and of the enforcement of
the Federal and Land laws, for example, for the reduction of odour
nuisances when liquid manure is being applied to the land.

The enforcement of the laws - also of Federal ones - is as a rule
incumbent upon the Länder which resort to their own authorities and to
municipal and regional administrations. The Federation has enforcement
agencies of its own for only a few specialised fields, which in any case
do not include water management, application of plant protection
products and nature and landscape protection.

Generally speaking, the legal situation on a regional level does not differ as greatly as might be imagined; in the majority of cases there is very little difference. This is also due to the fact that the Länder and the territorial authorities cooperate in the field of legislation, for instance, by elaborating model laws and model bylaws.

II. Regulations on manuring, application of plant protection products and consolidation (enlargement of ploughland and soil drainage)

A) Application of manure, sewage sludge and mineral fertilisers

Up until 1982 the application of manure (liquid manure, semi-liquid manure and stable manure), sewage sludge and mineral fertilisers was subject to legal restrictions in two respects only:

- the composition and labelling of mineral fertilisers under the Fertiliser Law of 1977
- manuring in the drainage basins of those 48 per cent of water catchment facilities (reservoirs, wells)*, for which a "water protection zone" had been identified within the scope of a formal procedure by statutory order.

The detection of heavy metal contents in sewage sludge then first entailed the issuing of the Regulation on Sewage Sludge. The increasing nitrate content in the groundwater of various regions led in 1982 to considerations as to how adequate are the general regulations now in force on the protection of groundwater and soil for the solution of this additional new problem on a legal basis. Details of the legal situation are as follows:

The Fertiliser Law (Duengemittelgesetz) stipulates that fertilisers may not be commercially marketed, unless they are in accordance with a generally approved type of fertiliser. Consequently, not every single fertiliser has to be registered. The list of approved fertiliser types is included in the Regulation on Fertilisers (Duengemittel-Verordnung), which also comprises labelling and packaging provisions. The approved

* 1982 figure

fertiliser types must not affect soil productivity, nor must they harm
human health or the health of domestic animals or endanger the natural
ecosystem, when properly used. They must promote the growth of useful
plants, increase their yields and improve their quality. The Fertiliser
Law does not provide for the use of fertilisers.

Example:

Type designation	Minimum contents	Type-determining constituents, nutrient forms, nutrient solubilities	Assessment; further requirements	Composition; type of manufacturing
		Mineral single nutrient fertilisers		
		Nitrogenous fertilisers		
Calcium magnesia nitrate	13% N 5% MgO	Nitrate nitrogen; water-soluble magnesium oxide	Nitrogen rated as nitrate nitrogen; magnesium content in water-soluble salts expressed as magnesium oxide	Calcium nitrate, magnesium nitrate

As already mentioned, fertilising can be restricted in "water
protection zones" (Wasserschutzgebiete according to Art. 19 of the Water
Management Law - Wasserhaushaltsgesetz). The identification of a water
protection zone is, inter alia, possible if it is necessary to protect
waters from detrimental effects in the interest of an existing or a
potential public water supply. In order to protect groundwater or
surface water in a reservoir, certain activities may be prohibited or
restricted by a decree issued by Länder authorities.

Usually the regulations on protection zones (which in 1982 covered only 48 per cent of nearly 14,000 water catchment facilities) prohibit, in accordance with the guidelines of the Deutscher Verein des Gas- und Wasserfaches e.V. - DVGW (German Association of Gas and Water Experts), only in very general terms "overfertilisation by organic fertilisation" and "improper application of mineral fertilisers". Concrete restrictions (for instance, as to a certain amount of nitrogen per hectare and per annum) are so far the exception.

The increasing nitrate content even in protected water reserves shows that this general restriction is insufficient. Apart from the identification of additional protection zones and financial aids for the construction of liquid manure tanks (which is already carried out by the Länder), absolute maximum limit values for nitrogen application should be fixed in protection zones (in my opinion 160 kg per hectare and per annum), and the keeping of an index file on ploughland as well as regular soil examinations should be made obligatory.

Even without a formal identification of a water protection zone, a restriction of manuring in the drainage basins of water catchment facilities would be possible according to the general provisions of water law. Fertilisation above a certain amount (for instance 160 kg N per hectare per annum) could, in accordance with Art. 2, 3, para 2 No.2 of the Water Management Law, be made conditional on a permit under the water law, since it is likely to cause harmful changes in the constitution of the water.

The application of manure, whether within or outside water protection zones, is subject to certain provisions of the Waste Disposal Law, to the extent that the "usual measure of agricultural fertilisation" is exceeded (Art. 15, para 1, sentence 2, Waste Disposal Law). In such cases the competent authority under the Land law may require the farmer to produce documentary evidence as to the type, quantity and application as well as to keep record books and retain and preserve supporting documents. This provision applies likewise to the application of sewage sludge and has so far only practical relevance in this area.

The "usual measure of agricultural fertilisation", which, if exceeded brings in strict official controls, is not the usual amount of applied fertilisers, but the amount which from a professional, agricultural standpoint is deemed necessary to achieve the desired purpose of soil cultivation.

In addition to the above-mentioned provisions, the Waste Disposal Law contains delegated powers to issue regulations on the selling and application of manure and sewage sludge. According to the wording of the law, which has been in force effectively since the amendment of 1982, the regulation can

1. restrict and prohibit the application according to criteria such as
   - pollutant content in the substance and in the soil
   - farm size
   - livestock
   - available surfaces and their exploitation
   - type and time of application and
   - natural site conditions
   and
2. make it dependent
   - upon an examination, disinfection or decontamination of these substances
   - upon compliance with certain quality requirements
   - upon the examination of the soil or
   - other suitable measures.

Corresponding regulations on the excessive use of fertiliser, incorporating restrictions on the application of manure are being prepared by the Länder. In Lower Saxony (Administrative Decree of 13 April 1983) and in Northrhine-Westphalia 240 kg per hectare per annum are considered as maximum values of normal fertilisation. The planned regulations (e.g. prohibition of application from late October to late February, construction of liquid manure tanks) concern only higher amounts than those shown above.

This provision of the Waste Disposal Law (Art. 15 in the version valid until 1982) was also the legal basis for the 1982 Regulation on Sewage Sludge. This Regulation has been issued to safeguard the agricultural utilisation of sewage sludge taking into account soil protection and hygienic concerns. For heavy metals such as lead, cadmium, chromium, copper, nickel, mercury and zinc, the values are fixed in the sewage sludge and in the soil; when these values are exceeded, sewage sludge may only be applied subject to approval by the competent authority. The soil and the sewage sludge must be regularly examined for contents of these substances (sewage sludge also for nitrogen, phosphate, potassium, calcium and magnesium). When the farmer takes delivery for application of the sludge, he receives a delivery note indicating the average heavy metal content (not the content for each single delivery) which has been detected.

The nitrate increase in groundwater observed in various regions has also entailed considerations as to the civil liability for improper fertilisation. The liability for damages for accidental water pollution without limitation to a maximum amount results from Art. 22 of the Water Management Law; legal proceedings and convictions on the basis of this provision have, however, not yet been brought in.

B)   Application of plant protection products

The farmer's selection of products is first of all restricted by the fact that plant protection products are subject to approval by the Biologische Bundesanstalt für Land- und Forstwirtschaft (Federal Biological Agency for Agriculture and Forestry).

The application of DDT (as well as its manufacture and distribution) is prohibited by the DDT Law and the application of 26 further active ingredients is prohibited by Annex 1 of the Ordinance on the application of plant protection products (Pflanzenschutzmittel-Anwendungsverordnung). Products containing these active ingredients are not granted approval.

The notification of approval also includes obligations relating to the products' labelling and packaging as well as to the wording of the instructions for use. The manufacturer and distributor may only advertise for the type of the approved application of the plant protection product.

For the farmer the instructions on use

    e.g. "no application next to water"

       "no application in the immediate vicinity of water

       (5-10 m distance to be allowed)"

are in the first instance not legally binding. In terms of liability law they may, however, represent the criteria of care, if a farmer is held liable for a concrete case of damage.

Apart from the above-mentioned prohibitions of application, the farmer may use plant protection products irrespective of the application for which the product is approved and regardless of whether it has any approval at all. The "proper application in accordance with instructions" is, however, according to the planned amendment of the plant protection law, to be made binding upon the farmer as "good professional practice".

In the first place, the above-mentioned regulation on the application of plant protection products is legally binding for the farmer. Apart from the prohibition of 26 active ingredients, it provides for restrictions on another 45 active ingredients. Quintozene, for instance, may only be applied for the treatment of cereal seeds, with the exception of maize, and seed potatoes. A vast majority of the restrictions concerns water protection. Many products may, for instance, only be applied with the consent of the agricultural and water authorities, even in the outer zones of water protection areas.

Furthermore, the farmer must comply with the regulation on Maximum Amounts for Plant Protection Products (Pflanzenschutzmittel-Höchstmengenverordnung) which belongs to the provisions of the Law on Foodstuffs. This regulation fixes the maximum amounts of active ingredients of plant protection products for foodstuffs of animal and vegetable origin. It forces the farmer to apply the products in accordance with instructions and to observe the waiting periods between the last application and the harvest.

The maximum contents for feedstuffs is controlled by the regulation on Feedstuffs (Futtermittelverordnung), which is based on the Law on Feedstuffs.

In formally identified water protection zones the following prohibitions apply in accordance with the guidelines of the German Association of Gas and Water experts (DVGW): in the restricted zone I, the application of all chemical plant protection products; in the remaining zones II and III, the application of soil and water-polluting products as well as of all products applied by spraying from aeroplanes. As a practical aid a list is available including the products whose approval has been subject to water protection obligations as well as a list of products which are recognised as safe in water protection zones.

The restrictions on use under the Nature and Countryside Protection Law remain to be pointed out. The Nature and Countryside Protection Laws of the Länder, which complete the framework law of the Federation, prohibit or restrict in different formulations the application of plant protection products on certain (abstractly described) surfaces or in general, outside of plots exploited for the purposes of agriculture and forestry (e.g. Art. 17 Nature and Countryside Protection Law of Baden-Württemberg, Art. 64, para 1, No.1, Countryside Law of Northrhine-Westphalia).

For the nature conservation zones, protected landscape components (and other territorial categories under Section IV of the Federal nature and Countryside Protection Law), prohibitions and restrictions may also be issued with a view to the application of plant protection products.

C) Ploughland enlargement and soil drainage

The most comprehensive procedure for the enlargement of ploughland, the consolidation of landed property and the improvement of the soil is offered by the Farmland Consolidation Law of 1953. To achieve these purposes, the Farmland Consolidation Proceedings include all agricultural surfaces in a specific area. In addition, the Proceedings cover the infra-structure: the re-routing and improving of roads, streets and waterways, and a lowering of the groundwater level effected by drainage, can be taken as two examples. These measures and consequently the whole range of farmland consolidation are only possible in coordination with representatives of those concerned (Art. 41, Farmland Consolidation Law). Farmland consolidation including road and water engineering has been carried out by means of large sums drawn almost exclusively from tax receipts and for this reason, it has frequently resulted in a complete reshaping of the areas involved. So far about one third of the agricultural surface in the Federal Republic of Germany has been restructured. The criticism that farmland consolidation impairs nature and landscape protection, because it tends to remove small woodlands and promote extensive soil drainage, led to the amendment of the Farmland Consolidation Law in 1976. This amendment allowed nature and countryside protection to be taken account of more effectively in new proceedings. At present it is even being considered whether the Farmland Consolidation Proceedings might also be applied for the enforcement of the restoration of uncultivated surfaces along roads and waters (border biotopes) in featureless "emptied" landscapes.

The general prohibition relating to the removal of hedges, trees and bushes depends on the interpretation of the Nature and Countryside Protection laws of the Federation and of the Länder. According to Art. 8, paras 1 and 2 of the Federal nature and Countryside Protection law, measures which considerably impair the availability of natural habitats or the characteristics of the landscape are prohibited. According to Art. 8, para 7, this prohibition does not, however, apply to "proper agricultural soil exploitation". The lawyers do not agree on the correct interpretation of this prohibition. According to the prevailing opinion the farmers are, therefore, exempted from the above-mentioned prohibition.

Small woodlands along roads and waters, which are of particular significance for the protection of wild animals and plants, might be removed from the farmers' reach as "protected landscape components" in accordance with Art. 18 of the Federal Nature and Countryside Protection Law. However, the Länder, which are competent in this matter, have so far only rarely made use of this provision.

The construction of drainage channels and the laying of drainage are not only carried out within the scope of the Farmland Consolidation Proceedings. These measures, which are considered as being partly responsible for an increase in washing-off of soil and flooding, do not require permits by virtue of a special provision in Art. 33, para 1 of the Water Management Law. According to water laws of the Länder (e.g. Art. 44, Water Law of Northrhine-Westphalia) they might, however, be made dependent on a permit under water law for individual areas.

III. Assessment

A) The assumption can generally be taken as correct that the German provisions correspond to the EC Directives.

B) The plant protection law and possibly also the exemption clauses for agriculture under the Federal Nature and Countryside Protection Law are, inter alia, to be amended.

Furthermore, I consider that it would be useful to introduce an amendment of the Nature and Countryside Protection Law which makes good agricultural practice of soil cultivation binding. Delegated powers for the introduction of soil-protecting limit values should not be provided, unless the determination of these values appears to be useful in terms of natural sciences.

Further amendments to the legislation are, in my opinion, unnecessary. For the solution of existing problems (e.g. nitrate in groundwater), the existing regulations provide sufficient grounds for taking action.

THE IMPACT OF ENVIRONMENTAL LEGISLATION UPON AGRICULTURE
The de jure situation in the United Kingdom

Philip Critchley
Department of the Environment, London

I must first of all make it clear that in presenting this paper I am not stating an official position but giving my own views. If I may say so, you have set yourselves a demanding goal: I shall do my best to fulfil my task and to outline, as succinctly as I can, the main features of our domestic environmental legislation as it affects agriculture.

May I begin, though, with a general observation. We hear a great deal these days about the effects of agriculture on the countryside. The conference theme turns the equation subtly round: here the subject is the impact of environmental law on agriculture itself. I think it is very useful to look from this other end of the telescope and to remind ourselves - since it is often overlooked - the extent to which existing legislation does already impinge on farming. It must, I believe, dispel any facile notion that developments in environmental control have somehow bypassed the agricultural sector.

Of course, I recognise that some argue that there should be more legislation: that is another matter, to which I shall return later.

Let me, then, now look in some detail at the relevant Acts; and Town and Country Planning legislation - principally embodied in the Town and Country Planning Act 1971 and associated orders - is a good starting-point. Our planning system aims to balance the protection of the natural and the built environment with pressure for economic and social change: it sets quality and amenity against the need to allow economic activity, including agriculture, without undue restrictions. Here, of course, we are looking at the issue from two angles: the protection which the Act gives to farming, to protect agricultural land from urban and other encroachment; secondly limitations on agriculture imposed by planning law.

I do not want to say too much about the first objective which falls, perhaps, outside of the mainstream of my talk. I would only make the point that the Government reaffirmed its commitment to preserve good agricultural land and to protect the countryside in DOE Circular 22/80 - "Development Control - Policy Practice" - which stated:

"Nor will the Government allow more than the essential minimum of agricultural land to be diverted to development, nor land of a higher agricultural quality to be taken where land of a lower quality could reasonably be used instead."

The recent draft circular on Green Belts contains a similar reference.

There is also, I should add, statutory provision requiring local planning authorities to consult the Ministry of Agriculture, Fisheries and Food where a proposed development is not in accordance with the provisions of a development plan and will result in the loss of not less than 10 acres of agricultural land either immediately or as a result of likely further development.

So one impact of planning law on farming is to safeguard its vital resource: the land. But how far does it affect what farmers do with that land?

The need for planning permission, and hence the extent of development control, is governed by Section 23 of the 1971 Act. This provides that anything within the definition of development set out in Section 22 requires planning permission - either the general permission given to many minor developments by the General Development Order, or, if it is not permitted development under the GDO, a specific permission from the local planning authority following a planning application to that body.

Generally, 'development' is defined as meaning the "carrying out of building, engineering, mining or other operations" on land or the making

of any material change in the use of buildings or land. Section
22(2)(e) excludes from the definition of development altogether the use
of land and buildings for agriculture as defined, so that no permission
is needed to change from one kind of agriculture to another; nor is it
required for bringing land or buildings into agricultural use from some
other use, including uncultivated or ungrazed land such as woodland,
hedgerow or marsh. This exemption has been a feature of the planning
system since its introduction in 1947, in recognition of the vital
importance of agriculture to the nation's economy.

Erection of buildings or engineering operations - such as
installing drains - for agriculture do, however, count as development.
But some of them will be covered by the provisions of the General
Development Order (Class VI of Schedule I) and will not need specific
planning permission. To benefit from these permitted development rights
the buildings or engineering operations must take place on agricultural
land (closely defined) of more than 1 acre and comprised in an
agriculture unit. They must be 'requisite for the use of that land for
the purposes of agriculture'. Dwellings, or any buildings or extensions
larger than 465 sq metres are not covered (recently erected buildings in
the same units count towards this total), nor those over 12 metres high
(3 metres near airfields), nor outbuildings or engineering operations
within 25 metres of classified roads. These provisions have also
remained substantially unchanged since the introduction of the planning
system. They have not been affected by EC directives. The wording of
Class VI has, I should add, been subject to successive legal
interpretations, with resultant confusion.

It is, however, open to a local planning authority to seek to
remove permitted development rights from any proposed development
including developments under Class VI, under Article 4 of the GDO,
subject to confirmation by the Secretary of State.

As to possible further legislation you will wish to take note that
DOE has recently published two consultation papers affecting Class VI
and agricultural building and operations. Between them they propose:

- First, replacement of the test I have described centred on the
  term "requisite ...... for the purposes of agriculture". We
  want to provide a clearer form of words less open to legal
  wrangles, but with broadly similar scope.

- Second, no further GDO right for new livestock buildings or
  extensions, or associated slurry stores, within 100 metres of
  residential or similar premises: for example hospitals and
  schools. This reflects the Government's recognition that the
  noise, smell and general intrusion generated by many intensive
  livestock units are disturbing to many people.

- Third, removal of GDO rights for engineering operations which
  comprise the tipping of waste brought onto the agricultural
  unit, or the excavation and removal of material from the unit.

If brought into effect, these changes would, accordingly, represent
some tightening-up of one or two aspects of present arrangements. Once
consultation is complete, the Department intends to lay an amending
order before Parliament as soon as possible.

Even so, you will readily see that direct planning controls on
agriculture would remain limited in scope. This is, of course, one of
the major sources of controversy in the countryside today. Critics of
present policies argue that the lack of such controls has been a major
contributory factor in the changes which the countryside has seen as new
'industrial' techniques of farming have been applied. The litany is
familiar: loss of habitats, hedgerows, trees and other landscape
features; drainage of wetlands of national and indeed international
importance.

The Government, on the contrary, takes the view that there are
strong arguments against the imposition of widespread planning controls
on agriculture. Obvious objections include cost, complexity, problems
of definition and where to draw the line, increased bureaucracy, and
even the seasonal nature of farming. But there is another factor too:
having a healthy countryside depends above all on good management by

people on the spot. It is essential, therefore, that we secure the active cooperation of the farming community to achieve conservation goals.

For that reason, Ministers have placed their faith in a voluntary approach to conservation, based on the offer, by conservation authorities (that is National Park Authorities, the Nature Conservancy Council and local planning authorities generally) of management agreements by which farmers are encouraged in the interests of conservation to accept restrictions on the way they farm their land - usually in return for payments reflecting the profits they have foregone.

It is at this point - where planning leaves off - that countryside legislation takes over. The Wildlife and Countryside Act 1981 reflected the voluntary approach and provided local authorities, for the first time, with general powers to offer agreements. (The Nature Conservancy Council already had such a power under earlier legislation.)

Though I must emphasise that there is no obligation on individual farmers to accept such agreements, the 1981 Act did introduce as well a number of actual constraints on farming operations - particularly those affecting land in Sites of Special Scientific Interest. In particular the owner or occupier of such land is now obliged to give 3 months' notice of any operation which he wishes to carry out which has been specified by the nature Conservancy Council as likely to damage the site. (As a concomitant of this the NCC is required, under the Act, to notify owners or occupiers of proposed designation of an SSSI, and to consider any representations made.) In some circumstances too, Nature Conservation Orders may be made by the Secretary of State delaying commencement of farmers' operations for up to 12 months.

The object of these clauses providing for delay is, of course, to allow time for negotiation of management agreements and the Act states that payments made under such agreements must be in accordance with guidance issued by Ministers. These guidelines were, in fact, published a year ago - and are, as some of you will know, a source of continuing controversy, largely because they reflect the principle that a farmer should not suffer any loss because he has entered into an agreement.

The 1981 Act also provides a special regime in National Parks,
SSSIs and other areas which may be specified from time to time, for the
consideration, by Agriculture Ministers, of applications for farm
capital grants. Ministers must consider any objection to such an
application made by the NCC, National Park or any other relevant
authority on the grounds that the work proposed would be environmentally
damaging. If Ministers decide to refuse the grant as a result of the
objection, the NCC or authority is, in these circumstances, obliged to
offer a management agreement to a farmer - again on the basis of the
Ministers' financial guidelines.

Other implications for agriculture of the 1981 Act are the reserve
power it provides for Ministers to designate areas of moor or heath in
National Parks to restrict agricultural operations, and the duty placed
on water authorities and internal drainage boards to further
conservation in exercising their functions. They are also now required
to consult the Nature Conservancy Council before carrying out operations
likely to be damaging in areas which the NCC has indicated are of
special interest.

I have centred my remarks on the 1981 Act because that is the most
recent advance. I have not time to do more than sketch out the broad
shape of earlier countryside legislation. However, in passing, let me
just note that the founding statute was, and is, the National Parks and
Access to the Countryside Act 1949 which, among other things,
established the National Parks Commission (later the Countryside
Commission) with powers to designate National Parks and Areas of
Outstanding Natural Beauty and also provided for the creation of
National Nature Reserves and areas of special scientific interest.
Here, of course, at that time the implications for agriculture were
essentially indirect. But later, the Countryside Act 1968 introduced
two major provisions with more immediate consequences for farming
activity.

First, Section 11 placed a general responsibility on Ministers,
Government Departments and public bodies "to have regard to the
desirability of conserving the natural beauty and amenity of the

countryside". The term conservation of natural beauty is defined in the Act as including references to flora, fauna and geological and physiographical features.

The very generality of its wording allows for great scope in interpreation, and has led to marked differences of emphasis between individual bodies and at different times as the political climate has changed. However, Departmental advice to local authorities since 1977 (DOE Circular 108/77) has been that authorities should take full account of conservation factors in formulating structure and local plans and in the consideration of individual planning applications.

The Act also contained a parallel provision, Section 37, which requires Ministers, local authorities, NCC and the Countryside Commission to have due regard to the needs of agriculture and forestry and to the economic and social interests of rural areas.

The effect of these two powers on agriculture cannot, of course, be directly quantified but 16 years after their enactment I would argue that they have contributed in no small measure to greater awareness in making land-use decisions - both of the importance of agriculture and forestry as industries of national importance and of the effect which those industries can have on the environment. They therefore represent a very real benefit to the quality of decision making.

I should just add that the Nature Conservancy Council was established by the Nature Conservancy Council Act 1973.

Let me now change tack. Planning and countryside law form one half of the picture. But, of course, there is a vital area of legislation dealing directly with pollution and public health which also has potential implications for farming - though, naturally, most of the Acts concerned are aimed much more widely and, in most cases, agriculture is not the main target. I want now to look at these in turn.

The safeguarding of water quality is, of course, a key feature of many of the Acts and clearly farming operations can have particular implications affecting that objective.

For example, under the Water Act 1945 authorities can make byelaws for the purpose of preventing pollution to their underground or surface water. Under Section 21 it is an offence to pollute springs, wells or adits used for the provision of water for human consumption. However in this case there is a saving to the effect that this shall not be held to restrict "any method of cultivation of land which is in accordance with the principles of good husbandry".

The Rivers (Prevention of Pollution) Acts 1951-61 took matters a stage further. Under these Acts it is an offence to cause or knowingly permit poisonous, noxious or polluting matter to enter inland waters. Here, it should be noted, there is no special protection for people who cause such pollution by carrying out normal agricultural activities. The Acts also require that discharges of trade or sewage effluents (and farm effluents are classed as trade effluent) must be the subject of consent by the water authority before they can be made to inland waters. Conditions regulating such matters as the nature and composition of the effluent may be imposed. There is a right of appeal to the Secretary of State against refusal of consent or unreasonable conditions.

The Clean Rivers (Estuaries and Tidal Waters) Act 1960 partially extended these controls to specified tidal rivers and estuaries.

I was asked to say a word or two about the Public Health Acts. Two of the relevant measures are concerned with regulating discharges of trade effluent to public sewers, and farm drainage comes within the meaning of trade effluent. Farmers may therefore discharge farm effluent to a sewer provided they have the consent of the water authority and comply with any conditions imposed. These conditions may include charges. There is a right of appeal to the Secretary of State against refusal or the terms of any condition imposed. However most farm effluents are too polluting to be accepted into a public sewer.

The Water Resources Act 1963 added again to the extent of protection provided to water supplies. Under this Act it is an offence to discharge liquid waste (trade and sewage effluent and any other poisonous, noxious or polluting matter) to underground strata, by means of any well, pipe or borehole, without the consent of the water authority. As with earlier Acts, conditions may be attached to consents, including precautions to be taken to prevent pollution of underground water, and there is a right of appeal to the Secretary of State.

We now come to the Control of Pollution Act 1974. Part II of this Act relates to water pollution. This Part has not hitherto been implemented but a phased programme of implementation is now under way. Certain transitional measures will apply to existing uncontrolled discharges. When fully implemented the Act will replace and repeal much of the earlier legislation - extending coverage to provide full control over inland, tidal and underground waters. Under Part II there are two offence provisions: the first concerns casual entries of poisonous, noxious or polluting matter; the second concerns regular discharges of trade or sewage effluent made without the consent of the water authority. Consent is required not only for such discharges made to relevant waters but also discharges from buildings or plant into or onto land, since substances discharged to land may find their way into water. The Act does, however, recognise the special position of agriculture and affords some protection to farmers by introducing the concept of codes of good agricultural practice, which provide a defence in that a person shall not be guilty of causing pollution if a polluting entry arises because of an act or omission undertaken in accordance with such practice. Some practices may be defined in a code approved by Agriculture Ministers for the purpose of the Act, but without prejudice to any other practice being good agricultural practice. Drafts were issued for comment on 7 February and cover such things as the application of organic and inorganic fertilisers and use of pesticides.

There is provision in the Act for this protection to be withdrawn in specific instances where pollution occurs or is likely to occur and the water authority may request the Secretary of State to serve notice on the farmer asking him to prevent acts or omissions of this kind. When such a notice is served the farmer's protection is withdrawn after 28 days and he will no longer be able to invoke the defence of acting in accordance with good agricultural practice if he is prosecuted.

Incidentally the defence provided by the code cannot be used in connection with discharges of effluent: these require consent even if they result from normal farming activities.

When implemented Part II will provide the means to comply with various EEC Directives concerned with protection of water. Those which are of most relevance in the agricultural context are No. 78/659/EEC (quality of fresh waters), No. 75/440/EEC (quality of surface water intended for abstraction of drinking water) and No. 80/68/EEC (dangerous substances into groundwater).

May I, at this point, say a brief word about the other Parts of the Control of Pollution Act, which are now, in large measure, in force.

Part I deals with waste. Most of the controls provided for in this Part of the Act reflect a number of relevant EC Directives. They relate predominantly to "controlled waste", which is defined as household, industrial and commerical waste. Waste from premises used for agriculture within the meaning of the Agriculture Act 1974 is specifically excluded from the definition of commercial waste, and, thereby, from the definition of controlled waste. However the Secretary of State, under Section 18(1), has power to make regulations to apply prescribed provisions of Part I to farm waste and, in addition, Section 18(2) makes it an offence to dispose, on any land, of any uncontrolled waste - including waste from agricultural premises - which is poisonous, noxious or polluting, in such a way as is likely to give rise to an environmental hazard.

The pollution problems posed by various forms of farm waste were one of the problems examined by the Royal Commission on Environmental Pollution in their seventh report - "Agriculture and Pollution" - to which the Government issued its response in December. One proposal the Commission made was that where disposal of chemical wastes took place off the farm these should be treated as controlled waste under Part I of the 1974 Act, and that some "intermediate provision" should govern disposal on the farm. However the Government is not at present satisfied that additional controls are necessary in view of the provisions of Section 18(2) to which I have referred.

Of course, rather as in the planning system, there is another
aspect to controls over waste: the protection of good quality farmland
from use for non-agricultural waste disposal. For example, in 1982,
some 2250 acres of farmland were being used for this purpose, or about
8 per cent of the total area of land used for landfill waste disposal in
England. DOE guidance is that good quality farmland should be released
for this purpose only when all reasonable alternatives have been
considered and rejected and all available relevant plans have been taken
into full account.

Parts III and IV of the Act relate to Noise and Atmospheric
Pollution. In Part III there is provision to enable local authorities
and individuals to take action where noise amounts to a statutory
nuisance. So, for example, the Act could be used to deal with noise
nuisance from audible bird scarers which are often used on farms
nowadays, and the subject of growing complaints from neighbours.

Part IV - atmospheric pollution - does not affect agriculture. It
is concerned largely with implementing EC legislation on sulphur in gas
oil and lead in petrol, and also gives local authorities a discretionary
power to require information from industry about air pollution
emissions.

In conclusion, I now turn to a mixed grill of other Acts which have
potential implications for agriculture. One important measure is
another Public Health Act - the Act of 1936 - which allows local
authorities and individuals to seek action to abate, mitigate or prevent
the recurrence of certain statutory nuisances.

Where agriculture is concerned the most obvious application of the
nuisance powers is to activities such as the keeping of livestock,
particularly in concentrations, and the burning off of straw and crops
stubble on fields at the end of the harvest season.

For example, the spreading of pig slurry on fields as a means of
disposal and fertiliser would be subject to the nuisance provisions
where offensive or noxious smells were generated.

Public health legislation also applies to other activities, such as the processing of animal wastes. Such plants can create substantial smell problems leading to pressures on local authorities to call for remedial measures. Although by no means ineffective, the legislation in some respect does require updating and tightening up to meet present day conditions. The Department has therefore been reviewing this legislation but final decisions have yet to be taken.

We all recall, of course, the controversy of last summer caused by straw and stubble burning. The smoke and smuts produced by such burning can cause severe problems of nuisance as well as serious fire damage and other undesirable effects. Clean air legislation extends local authorities' statutory nuisance powers to control this type of activity (though in practice, unlike smell nuisance, it is often hard to identify the particular source of smoke nuisance or consequently to take effective remedial action). In conjunction with the Home Office and the Ministry of Agriculture, the Department has been examining ways in which to strengthen control of burning by extending the scope of existing provisions of local authority byelaws on the subject. New proposals are intended to limit the concentration of burning in one area at any one time, to provide wider firebreak requirements, and to minimise the potential for smut nuisance by requiring incorporation into the soil of ash and other burnt residue within a limited time. It is hoped that revised model byelaws will be available to local authorities in time for this year's burning season. Farmers will have to comply with any such byelaws or face heavy fines.

Among the other points I was asked to cover today were included some rather more obscure Acts and Regulations, for example, the Salmon and Freshwater Fisheries Act 1975. Under Section 4 of that Act - which could have implications for farming in some circumstances - it is an offence to put any liquid or solid matter into any waters containing fish which would cause injury to those fish.

Then there is the Farm and Gardens Chemical Act 1967. However this probably lies rather outside my immediate scope since its purpose, with associated regulations, is to impose requirements on the labelling and marketing of certain products such as weedkillers. There are also the

Fertiliser and Feeding Stuff Regulations and I should note here that a number of EC Directives deal with animal feeding stuffs. As a result most feed additives are subjected to an EC approval process and any possible effects on the environment are carefully evaluated before approval is given. UK legislation is amended from time to time to mirror the provisions of Directives enacted in Brussels.

Lastly, I should mention the Health and Safety (Agriculture) (Poisonous Substances) Regulations 1975. These regulations impose obligations to protect agricultural operators from poisoning by the more dangerous compounds by ensuring, among other things, that they wear adequate protective clothing when working with the substances listed in the regulations. These regulations are, in fact, about to be updated to cover new substances developed, and a new guidance booklet produced. I am told the old one found its way as far afield as Canada and Australia.

That concludes my résumé of some of the relevant legislation. I do not pretend it is a complete survey and you will appreciate that I am not, personally, an expert on all the Acts and Regulations named.

At this point the guidance sent me earlier suggested some "assessment by the speaker" might not come amiss. For example, how well does our existing legislation cover the possible pollution and environmental damage caused by agriculture? Some suggestions were also requested as to possible improvement in environmental legislation. This, of course, is sensitive ground for a civil servant and apart from the passing comments I have made at one or two points already, I think it would be right for me to leave such questions principally for others to pursue. However, in case you think I am ducking the problem altogether, may I just make one observation which I believe is an important one: namely, that legislation is only one aspect of systems of control or management. Let me explain what I mean. I have already, for example, drawn attention to the way in which countryside legislation relies heavily on encouraging voluntary methods of conservation. We can see a similar non-statutory element at work in some other important areas as well.

The same principle has been applied for many years to pesticides, for example with the Advisory Committee on Pesticides - ACP - which, as the Government response to the Seventh Report of the Royal Commission on Environmental Pollution said: "has provided independent advice to successive Administrations for nearly 30 years and the Government intend that it shall continue to do so"; and, again, the Pesticides Safety Precautions Scheme - a non-statutory arrangement between government departments and the relevant industrial associations, to ensure that new pesticides or new uses for pesticides are not introduced without prior clearance for environmental safety.

The point is, I think, sufficiently made. It is part of the tradition in our country that we do not seek a legislative solution where a non-statutory means of proceeding is available. It reflects, if you like, our national way of life. We prefer, wherever we can, to allow more informal arrangements to operate, based on consensus and mutual agreement. Of course, there will always be arguments where precisely the dividing line between this type of approach and a supporting legislative framework should be drawn. That is in the nature of things.

Here I bring my remarks to a close. As I say, I am only too conscious of my omissions. My brief reference, at one or two points, to the Royal Commission on Environmental Pollution and its report on agriculture and pollution could certainly form the subject of a talk in its own right.

THE IMPACT OF ENVIRONMENTAL LEGISLATION UPON AGRICULTURE
The de jure situation in the EEC

Nigel Haigh
Institute for European Environmental Policy

Despite being only 10 years old, EC environmental policy has resulted in a considerable body of legislation which has had effects in all Member States though they differ from one to another. The field selected for initial attention by the EC Commission has to a large extent been the traditional one of industrial pollution and the effects on agriculture of this legislation is often minimal – although some may have increasing implications over time. Indeed, a study of EC environmental legislation is unlikely to prove the best point of departure for a study of agriculture and the environment in a Community context – a subject which is at last attracting the attention it deserves. One may speculate on the reasons for this.

Bureaucracies draw demarcation lines for the purposes of administrative convenience, and in the EC, as elsewhere, distinctions are drawn between agricultural measures and environmental measures. Ten years ago in the first Action Programme on the Environment[1] the Commission "expressed its intention of increasing its campaign in the future for the protection of the natural environment and particularly within the framework of the agricultural policy". These words recognise that a demarcation line has to be crossed. In fact the two principal products of that 'campaign', the birds Directive (79/409[2]) and the less favoured areas (LFA) Directive (75/268[3]), lie on opposite sides of the line. Whereas both Directives are concerned with protecting habitats and countryside, the birds Directive is regarded as an environmental measure while the LFA Directive is regarded as an agricultural measure. It is largely for its narrow agricultural base that the LFA Directive is now criticised by environmental bodies and why efforts are being made to amend it. This significant development is surely the better point of departure for a study of agriculture and the environment in a Community context – but is outside the terms of reference of this paper. The need to bridge our artificially created demarcation lines was recognised in the Council declaration approving the Third Action Programme[4]. It spoke of the need to 'integrate the environmental dimension into other policies'. EC environmental legislation consists of between 70 and 100 Directives, Regulations and Decisions (depending on what one counts). These can be conveniently divided into 35 groups under six broad headings (water, waste, air, chemicals, wildlife, noise). Only a few of these impinge on agriculture and only these are discussed here. Summaries and formal details (including dates for compliance) of all these Directives are to be found in my book "EEC Environmental Policy and Britain - An Essay and a Handbook"[5].

Noise

Member States may not set more stringent noise limits for tractors than those specified in two Directives[6]. Chain saws are not yet the subject of EC legislation although they were mentioned in the First Action Programme.

Waste

A broad framework for the control of waste and toxic waste is laid down in two separate Directives[7]. Agricultural waste is excluded from the waste Directive and 'animal carcases and agricultural waste of faecal origin' is excluded from the toxic waste Directive. However other agricultural waste such as contaminated drums or bags of pesticides are not excluded, to my knowledge.

Air

One Directive[8] sets air quality standards for smoke and sulphur dioxide and another[9] sets air quality standards for lead in air. Another Directive[10] limits lead in petrol. A series of Directives[11] limits the freedom of Member States to impose more stringent standards than those specified for vehicle emissions (including smoke emitted by tractors). These Directives were not drawn up with a view to protecting agriculture but primarily to protecting human health. It is also doubtful whether they have influenced agricultural practices - even straw burning, which is a source of intense smoke, covers such short periods that it is not likely to cause a breach of the smoke Directive

which averages out the amount of smoke over a period of several months.
However, the reduction of smoke, sulphur dioxide and lead in a European
context must be beneficial to agriculture.

Water

The water Directives fall into two categories: those which set
water quality objectives for certain uses of water (bathing[12],
drinking[13], fish life[14]) and those which control the discharge of
dangerous substances from point sources to water and from point or
diffuse sources to groundwater. None of these Directives was introduced
to protect agriculture though if as a result rivers become cleaner they
will protect water abstracted for agricultural purposes. Agricultural
run off could affect the quality of water for freshwater fish set in the
relevant Directive[15] (although the nitrate parameter which existed in
the proposed Directive was deleted during negotiations under pressure at
least from the UK), and certainly affects the quality of water for
abstraction for drinking laid down in a Directive[16], and in the quality
of drinking water laid down in another Directive. Indeed the nitrate
parameter in the drinking water Directive is not completely met in most
EC Member States. The groundwater Directive[17] could also have a long
term influence on the application by farmers of nitrogenous fertilisers,
as nitrites are among the substances which the Directive says are not to
be indirectly discharged to groundwater.

Chemicals

The principal item of legislation in this field (known as the
'sixth amendment')[18] requires substances (including presumably some used
in agriculture) to be tested and notified for harmful effects before
they are marketed. There are also three groups of Directives dealing
with pesticides:

   a) four Directives fixing the maximum levels of pesticide residues
      in fruit and vegetables[19]
   b) two Directives relating to the labelling and packaging of
      pesticides[20]
   c) two Directives prohibiting the sale and use of plant protection
      products containing certain active substances[21].

There are also two Decisions restricting the use of chlorofluoro-
carbons and to the extent that these substances affect the ozone belt
which protects vegetation from ultraviolet radiation they are having a
beneficial effect on agriculture. The UK implements the pesticides
Regulations on a voluntary basis. Doubts about the adequacy of the
scheme have been voiced both in and outside the UK.

Wildlife

There are Regulations restricting the import of whole products and
products of other endangered species, but these do not affect
agriculture. The birds Directive on the other hand has the potential
for influencing agriculture and indeed is arguably the most powerful
weapon in the hands of those concerned with environmental policy in the
Community for piercing the demarcation line described above. The reason
for this is that in addition to protecting species of birds from certain
forms of killing and hunting it also lays a general duty on Member
States to preserve, maintain and re-establish a sufficient diversity and
area of habitats for all species of naturally occurring birds in the
wild state.

Thus if, as a result of the developments in technology or as a
consequence of agricultural policies or for any other reason, the
habitats of birds are so encroached upon as to threaten those birds then
there would be a breach of the obligations in the Directive. One can
thus see a potential conflict between Article 39 of the Treaty of Rome
with its emphasis on increasing productivity and the obligations of the
bird Directive.

The LFA Directive and the other agricultural structures Directives
fall outside the scope of this paper, despite the fact that the proposed
amendments to these Directives for environmental reasons among others
provides the most interesting development in the field of environment
and agriculture.

A recent development of possible long term significance is the
agreement by the Council of Ministers on 6 March to formalise an
embryonic Community environmental fund - known as ACE (Action by the
Community on the Environment). This provides a small sum of money for

the protection of habitats for birds - though as originally proposed it could have been used more generally for nature protection purposes. One reason why the Regulation embodying this new fund is restricted to habitats for birds is because of the lack of express provision in the Treaty of Rome for nature protection. This deficiency could well come to have increasing significance as the debate on environment and agriculture develops in a Community context.

References

Page 25

[1] First Action Programme on the Environment: OJ C112, 20.12.73

[2] Birds Directive (79/409): OJ L103, 25.4.79

[3] LFA Directive (75/268): OJ L128, 19.5.75

[4] Third Action Programme: OJ C46, 17.2.83

Page 26

[5] Published in February 1984 and available from Environmental Data Services Ltd, 40 Bowling Green Lane, London EC1R ONE

[6] Noise Directive (74/151): OJ L84, 28.3.74
                  (77/311): OJ L105, 28.4.77

[7] Waste Directive (75/442): OJ L194, 25.7.75
Toxic and Dangerous Waste Directive (78/319): OJ L84, 31.3.78

[8] Smoke and Sulphur Dioxide in Air Directive (80/779): OJ L229, 30.8.80

[9] Lead in Air Directive (82/884): OJ L378, 31.12.82

[10] Lead in Petrol Directive (78/611): OJ L197, 22.7.78

[11] Pollution from Motor Vehicles Directive:
        Petrol engines (70/220): OJ L76, 6.4.70
        Diesel engines (72/306): OJ L190, 20.8.72
        Tractors (77/537):   OJ L220, 29.8.77

Page 27

[12] Bathing Water Directive (76/160): OJ L31, 5.2.76

[13] Drinking Water Directive (75/440): OJ L194, 25.7.75
                    (80/778): OJ L229, 30.8.80

[14] Shellfish Water Directive (79/923): OJ L281, 10.11.79

[15] Water Standards for Freshwater
        Fish Directive (78/659):   OJ L222, 14.8.78

Page 27 (continued)

16 Dangerous Substances in

     Water Directive (76/464):   OJ L129, 18.5.76

17 Groundwater Directive (80/68):   OJ L20, 26.1.80

18 Sixth Amendment (79/831):   OJ L259, 15.10.79

19 Pesticide Residues Directives

     (i)   76/895:   OJ L340, 19.12.76

     (ii) 80/428:   OJ L102, 19.4.80

     (iii) 81/36:   OJ L46, 19.2.81

     (iv) 82/528:   OJ L234, 9.8.82

20 Labelling and Packing Directives

     (i)   78/631:   OJ L206, 29.7.78

     (ii) 81/187:   OJ L77, 2.4.81

21 Plant Protection Products Directives

     (i)   79/117:   OJ L33, 8.2.79

     (ii) 83/131:   OJ L91, 9.4.83

SESSION II

THE EFFECTIVENESS OF ENVIRONMENTAL LEGISLATION
The de facto situation in the UK

David Baldock
Institute of European Environmental Policy, London

The body of environmental legislation which affects agriculture in
the UK is diverse in form, content and intention and perhaps equally
varied in its application. Ideally, each law or code of practice should
be considered individually, although the evidence required for a full
assessment is often unavailable. This paper will not attempt anything
so ambitious but will have to rely on some broad generalisations and
personal impressions. The main focus will be on the laws designed to
protect the countryside which are currently attracting particular
interest.

The "effectiveness" of a law may be taken to mean a number of
things. Is it fully applied? Is it rigorously enforced? Has it had
any perceivable effects? Has it met its stated objectives? It is rare
for the consequences of a new law to be scrupulously monitored, but it
is possible to gain some impression of its impact from the number of
infringements reported, from court cases arising, from evident changes
in practice, from informed comment, etc.

The "effectiveness" of a law depends also on the viewpoint of the
observer. For example, in recent evidence to a House of Lords
Committee, the Ministry of Agriculture made it clear that they regarded
the UK's existing countryside protection legislation as broadly
adequate, whereas several environmental organisations expressed the
opposite view with some force.

Some UK legislation is extremely vague. Under Section 11 of the
Countryside Act 1968, every Minister, government department and public
body is obliged to have regard to the desirability of conserving the
natural beauty and amenity of the countryside in making their own
decisions. Such a formulation probably has little effect on any

individual decisions and has not prevented what many people would describe as a serious deterioration in the natural beauty of the countryside, but nonetheless it may have helped to establish a certain precedent and stimulate greater awareness of the issue amongst the agricultural authorities.

The changes in the countryside have raised much concern in the British public recently. In 1977 the Nature Conservancy Council produced its report on modern agriculture and the environment. They estimated that since 1949 more than 95 per cent of lowland herb-rich meadows have disappeared, or have been largely destroyed, with only 3 per cent remaining completely undamaged. About 50-60 per cent of the fernland and marshland in valley bottoms in the lowlands has vanished. The effect of agriculture on wildlife and the visual appearance of the countryside has been immense.

Perhaps the most significant aspect of environmental controls over agriculture is that so many are not enshrined in law. There is a marked tendency to favour a voluntary approach to environmental questions in the countryside, sometimes backed up by codes of practice. Examples include the Wildlife and Countryside Act, the NFU's straw burning code and the UK approach to pesticide controls. Such an approach usually works best when those concerned have a strong interest in following the code, but otherwise is vulnerable to abuse. The present government and the farming organisations tend to support the voluntary approach, while increasingly environmental groups are opposed to it. The effectiveness of the voluntary approach is increasingly doubtful. The voluntary Pesticides Safety Precautions Scheme was successful in reducing the environmental damaged caused by organochlorine pesticides, but its limitations have become increasingly clear and there is now strong pressure to make it statutory. Up to the present there is nothing to stop a farmer from buying and applying pesticides that have not been cleared. The 120 or so farm inspectors responsible for health and safety who police the application of pesticides cannot prevent abuse, as they can only visit a particular farm about once in five years on average. The straw burning code has not succeeded in controlling a growing number of incidents involving damage, annoyance and serious accidents. This too may become statutory. The largely voluntary

approach underlying the Wildlife and Countryside Act has encouraged many
farmers to co-operate, but many others have exploited the lack of
statutory controls and the loss of wildlife habitat has continued at a
rapid pace, with many SSSIs being destroyed in the process. Since the
Act came into force, 15 SSSIs have been damaged and a further 7 proposed
SSSIs have been partly destroyed. Notwithstanding this experience, the
government is reported to be considering a new voluntary code on the use
of nitrogen fertilisers.

Pollution control legislation has largely exempted agricultural
practice up until now. Ten years after the Control of Pollution Act
1974 came into being, Section 31, which is of most relevance to
agriculture, is about to be implemented for the first time. This will
probably not have a great impact as polluting activities arising from
"good agricultural practice" will continue to be allowable.

Land use planning legislation has a central role in environmental
legislation in the UK, but its impact on agriculture has been limited.
There are some controls on farm buildings, but these are narrow in scope
and not always easy to enforce. More effective has been the
establishment of certain designated areas, such as the National Parks,
where local authorities and the statutory conservation bodies have a
greater role. Farmers are deeply opposed to the extension of planning
controls in the countryside, but this possibility is no longer remote.

The weakness of the present legislation and voluntary codes arises
not only from the limited legal powers available, but also from the lack
of financial resources available to conservation bodies. This is likely
to prove a particularly important factor in inhibiting the area which
can be protected under the provisions of the 1981 Wildlife and
Countryside Act.

To increase the effectiveness of environmental legislation, it is
necessary to extend its scope rather than to enforce existing law more
rigorously. Unfortunately, it is less clear whether this can be
achieved without determined opposition from the farming community.

THE EFFECTIVENESS OF ENVIRONMENTAL LEGISLATION
The de facto situation in the FRG

Rudolf Elsner

Bundesministerium für Ernährung, Landwirtschaft u. Forsten, Bonn

It is not easy to comment on the second topic of this very worthwhile seminar. The relevant environmental legislation in West Germany, the content of which has already been presented, is for the main part less than 10 years old, so that experience as regards its effectiveness is limited. An assessment of the situation is all the more difficult in that a large number of the necessary regulations for the practical implementation of the legislation date from an even more recent period. Furthermore, the assessment demanded for this topic is inevitably coloured - however hard one tries to be objective - by a subjective view.

How can "effectiveness" be measured?

This question is based on the assumption that legislation has a positive effect on the environment in those areas where agriculture and the environment might conflict. Basically this view is correct.

Certain limits are, however, imposed upon legislation as an instrument to stabilise and improve the environmental situation.

Bearing in mind these objectives, effective environmental legislation has as a first premise that the facts of the matter requiring regulation should be clear. This means that there should be no uncertainties or significant gaps in the knowledge of the facts concerning complicated ecological cause and effect processes in which agriculture is involved, for example, by use of chemicals. But up to now, unfortunately, we do not know enough about the results of human interference with nature's arrangements, or about the harmful effects, especially the long-term or the synergistic effects or the regenerative capacity of complete ecosystems. Because of these gaps in our knowledge it is a priori difficult to formulate regulations, which preserve the functional integrity of nature in all its different features, and secure its potential for productivity and regeneration. Legislation on a topic of this nature is a long-term task, which can only be carried out in small steps, and only insofar as research can provide the necessary data for decision making. It follows that environmental legislation needs constant adaptation to new scientific knowledge in order to be effective.

Furthermore, legislation which is effective in protecting the environment can only be achieved if the legislature brings to bear sufficient political will and power of implementation, and introduces into the legislation such measures as are deemed necessary against opposing interests, without coming to indefensible compromises at the expense of the environment. But regulations formulated along these lines are even then only effective if they are implemented consistently by the responsible experts. This is, in my opinion, an especially weak point, because the implementing authorities often do not have enough specialists in this new legal sphere who are able to recognise cases where intervention is required and who can then deal with such cases adequately by reason of their professional competence.

Finally, an effective environmental legislation presupposes the will to accept it by those who are concerned, because observation of the regulations cannot be supervised at all times and in all places. Such acceptance must be based upon a consciousness of the problem which has been developed by training and education, as well as upon legislation which also takes into account economic requirements.

Having made these comments on pre-conditions for an effective environmental legislation, I now want to elaborate on the question of how to measure the effectiveness of environmental legislation.

The most acceptable yardstick is the actual improvement in environmental conditions or at the very least a halt to deterioration in areas where agriculture is practised. To spell this out, it means that:

In spheres of activity from which the greatest dangers for the
environment derive, such as:
- use of pesticides
- fertilising
- farming of large consolidated areas, and land improvements
- emissions from harmful airborne substances and harmful substances
    from sewage sludge
further deterioration has been halted and better environmental
conditions have been achieved (or are expected in the near future) by
the preventive effect or the implementation of the relevant regulations.

How effective was environmental legislation in the various
activities listed?

What changes in the legislation could further improve the actual
condition of the environment?

Use of pesticides

The use of pesticides creates the following environmental problems:

- Wild plant and animal species are affected directly or indirectly
    due to reduction of their nutritional basis.

This is particularly the case with the use of broad spectrum
pesticides or with prophylactic treatments, or when pesticides are
applied directly or by spraying (especially from aircraft) to natural
habitats. A particular problem is caused by the use of non-selective
pesticides, whereby useful pest-killing species are damaged whose
elimination then leads to the use of even more pesticides.

- Repeated use causes resistance to pests and necessitates a
    constant replacement with newer plant protection varieties.

- Foodstuffs can be contaminated with residues from pesticides.

- It is true that direct damage to the soil and its micro-organisms
  has been ruled out by scientific investigations where pesticides
  are only used once a year, because of the high potential for
  regeneration by the micro-organisms; however, the effects of
  repeated treatments are still uncertain. Certain pesticides
  accumulate in the soil; even though no damaging effects can be
  deduced from this up to the present, this accumulation must be
  considered as serious. Impairments to the soil fauna have been
  observed frequently, and from these factors the manifold
  functions of the soil could be indirectly and negatively
  affected.

- The contamination of the air by pesticides has rarely been
  examined. It is known, however, that a considerable amount of
  pesticide becomes airborne.

- Other problems occur in drinking-water protection zones
  (endangering the quality of the drinking water) and with the
  introduction of pesticide residues into small areas of water
  (endangering of water fauna and flora).

The German plant protection law regulates mainly the licensing of
pesticides and only to a lesser degree their application. The
effectiveness of these legal regulations can therefore only be measured
by analysing the pesticides licensed for application in agriculture and
forestry.

The aim of the licence is not only to guarantee a useful remedy
against pests and weeds but also to keep the damage to man and the
environment as low as possible. It has to be admitted though that the
ecological objective has not been set out very clearly up till now in
the licensing regulations. Nevertheless, positive results have been
achieved from the ecological point of view. There is, for example, an
unmistakable trend towards the licensing of selective instead of broad
spectrum pesticides. The number of cases in which licences are
withdrawn, if their practical use creates unacceptable ecological
damage, is increasing. There is meanwhile a total prohibition on

26 substances (especially organochlorines and heavy metal compounds);
13 substances are only allowed for restricted use and
31 substances are under limited prohibition orders (especially for the
protection of water). Since 1972 DDT has been neither used nor produced
in West Germany. Furthermore, the law on plant protection and
foodstuffs has brought about a considerable reduction in the amount of
pesticide residues in, for example, vegetables, over the last few years.

Despite these results we have no doubt that further legislation
needs to be introduced to intensify ecotoxicological control and to
limit the use of pesticides to an ecologically defensible level.

These aims are served not only by the promotion of the so-called
integrated plant protection scheme but also by a key measure, which lies
outside the legal armamentarium, namely, a new plant protection law
which is being discussed at the moment in the Deutsche Bundestag
(Parliament) and which contains (inter alia) the following regulations:

1. The averting of dangers to nature arising from the use of
   pesticides is explicitly named as the object of the law.

2. Pesticides may only be used according to good professional
   practice and only in such a way that no damage (inter alia) to
   the natural world need be feared.

3. Pesticides may only be used on open land, if this is used for
   purposes of agriculture, forestry or horticulture. Their use
   is generally not allowed in or near water.

4. If there is any immediate danger the Federal Agricultural
   Minister can enact prohibitions or limitations for certain
   pesticides without obtaining the consent of the Bundesrat
   (Upper House).

5. For agricultural, forestry and professional users and for
   salesmen of pesticides, a certificate of certain personal
   standards and professional knowledge is to be introduced.

6. As well as the approval of the Federal Bureau of Health, the approval of the Federal Bureau of the Environment has to be obtained for the separate media of water, air and waste disposal before the pesticide can be licensed.

7. New types of plant protection equipment can only be allowed on the market if they conform to certain demands for the protection of man, animal and nature. The Länder are empowered to carry out checks on the use of certain types of plant protection apparatus.

Experiences with the implementation of the national plant protection law have persuaded the Federal Republic of Germany to work towards an increased consideration of ecological requirements in the harmonisation of plant protection laws in the European Community. This is the case, for example, in the draft Council-Directive on the marketing of EC licensed pesticides.

Pesticides are partly used to improve the quality standard in the appearance of agricultural products (especially, for example, of fruit). Lower quality standards could in some cases lead to a reduction in the use of pesticides. It might be possible to persuade the consumer to forego certain criteria of appearance if these criteria were given less importance in classifications, quality norms and standards. However, quality norms are enforced under EEC law and can therefore only be changed at European Community level. A reconsideration of type, scope and benefit of possible changes in quality norms would be advisable.

Fertilising

Environmental problems arising from fertilising are as follows:

- The leaching of nitrate into ground water on a considerable scale, both locally and regionally, which is mainly due to the intensive cultivation of various products (viticulture, horticulture) on permeable soils, and to very intensive livestock farming (more than 2 to 3 animal units per ha).

- Eutrophication of areas of water, especially small streams and ponds in rural areas due to the running-off of nutrients (especially phosphate and nitrogen) from cultivated soils; this has harmful effects upon the water fauna and flora and leads to a gradual silting up of the water area.

- Odours from the application of organic fertiliser close to housing areas and in regions with over-intensive animal production.

- Impairment of the living conditions of wildlife (animals and plants), especially in areas hitherto extensively used, such as rough grazing and hayfields.

- Excessive use of nitrogen fertiliser can produce unhealthy levels of nitrate accumulation in certain plants (e.g. spinach) or at least impair the quality (freshness, taste, content) of the crop.

The laws covering possible solutions to these problems are those relating to fertilisers, waste disposal, and water.

The law on fertilisers has brought about a situation whereby licences are only granted for types of mineral or mineral-organic fertilisers that will not endanger, inter alia, the ecological balance when used with a high standard of professional care (for example, by limiting the content of harmful components, especially heavy metals). But the law on fertilisers contains regulations only for the licensing and not for the application of fertilisers, so it offers no possibilities of action to prevent the excessive use of, for example, mineral nitrogen fertiliser in intensive cultivation with the resulting overload of nitrate in the ground water, or a critical nitrate accumulation in vegetables such as spinach. The considerable increase in nitrate content in the ground water of certain wine and vegetable-growing regions shows that the restrictions on fertiliser use enforced by the water law in the limited areas of the water protection zones are in themselves not sufficient to solve the problem.

Claims for compensation have very rarely been made under the S22 WHG (water supply law) on the basis of change in the physical, chemical or biological structure of the ground water resulting from nitrate contamination, mainly because the identification of the individual responsible for the damage and the proof of a causal link between fertilising and nitrate run-off is difficult to establish. To help find a solution to this problem (which will increase in importance once the EC drinking-water directive with its nitrate limit of 50 mg/l comes into force in 1985), discussions are currently in progress on increasing the range of identified water protection zones and - especially among the environmental lobby - on the introduction of a tax on mineral nitrogen fertiliser (limiting its use by increasing the price). Furthermore demands have been made for regulations on fertiliser application in the law relating to fertilisers, and also on the maximum permitted content of nitrate in vegetables under the law relating to foodstuffs.

The possibilities for intervention which were offered by the first version of the Waste Disposal Law to prevent the excessive use of organic fertilisers such as slurry have brought about a noticeable reduction in the number of cases of gross over-manuring, which were in reality cases of waste disposal. But they have not been able to prevent the increasing nitrate contamination of the ground water in regions with intensive animal production and light permeable soils.

In 1982 the law was changed in order to come closer to finding a solution to this problem by the use of legal instruments. Now the Bundesländer or the Landkreise (counties) can lay down regulations on the application and control of organic fertilisers, taking into account the special natural conditions of given regions. Furthermore the locally responsible administration can prohibit or limit the spreading of fertiliser on areas devoted to agriculture, forestry or horticulture in individual cases, if the normal scale of agricultural fertilising is exceeded, thereby contaminating the ground water or the surface water.

Some Bundesländer have already issued regulations on the application of fertilisers, or are preparing them. These contain, inter alia, regulations on the permitted quantities, and prohibitions on spreading during the winter season.

The regulations are already showing some effects. The farmers are starting to build larger slurry containers to cover a longer storage period. Furthermore, the organisation of a better system of slurry distribution between intensive animal production units and other farm units is under consideration, for example the creation of manure banks on a cooperative basis, using the example of the Dutch.

Cultivation of large fields and land improvements

Apart from the intensive use of agricultural land areas, the creation of larger fields and improvements such as land consolidation, drainage and road construction have also impaired or destroyed the habitats of wildlife (animals and plants), which should be protected for ethical, evolutionary and biological reasons but also for the reasons set out as follows:

- in order to provide a potential genetic reservoir in wildlife which will enable agricultural researchers to improve upon the genetic health of domestic plants and animals.

- in order to develop biological methods of pest eradication by the integration of pest-killing species, on account of the ecological and economic damage caused by excessive use of chemicals, which is in turn due to the increasing resistance of pests.

- in order to support biological self-purification, the stabilisation of the atmosphere and the water economy, the formation of humus and many other factors by means of ecosystems which can only be kept in balance through the existence of numerous animal and plant species.

The habitats of such animal and plant species have been impaired or destroyed by land consolidation, drainage and road building; natural or semi-natural areas such as hedges, field trees, field borders, waste land, uncultivated land, moors, ditches, ponds, pools, bogs, marshy meadows, litter meadows, pastures and scattered orchards have all been affected. The danger continues.

The enlarged field structure and the elimination of odd corners in their natural or semi-natural state increase erosion by wind and water, and the recreational and amenity value of the landscape deteriorates (reduction of variety).

For certain features, continued extensive agricultural use is the factor ensuring the support and protection of special biotopes (poor grassland, rough grazing, litter meadows, marshy meadows). The extensive use of such areas forms a positive contribution to the protection of the environment.

Since the mid-1970s the federal nature protection law (Bundesnaturschutzgesetz) and the nature protection laws promulgated by the Länder have helped to secure an important number of habitats for wildlife by the setting-up of nature reserves. However, protection under these regulations is only possible for certain areas in which special protection is necessary either for the natural world and the countryside as a whole, or for particular individual features, in order to maintain the existence of certain natural communities or habitats, for example, moors or heathland which are worth preserving. These regulations cannot, in general, guarantee the protection of valuable biotopes at the expense of measures to improve the efficiency of the agricultural structure.

To preserve valuable features of the countryside, and biotopes (or habitat types) however small, from encroachment as much as possible, the so-called basic concepts for grant-aid (based on the law) have been put forward in the communal document:

"Improvement of the agricultural structure and of coastal protection".

This paper declares that consideration should be given to the needs of environmental protection, conservation of nature and the countryside in the course of structural improvements in agriculture.

Initially, the ecological results of setting out these basic concepts were inconsiderable. This has changed in recent times, since various improvements in the restrictions were adopted and additional commitments established on an ecological basis at the annual discussion and review.

Of these, the following should particularly be mentioned:

- The fundamental exclusion from the granting of aids for measures which would or could change or considerably impair rare or valuable biotopes including their typical soil types; for land consolidation processes as well as measures affecting cultivation and drainage, this prohibition has been elaborated and given more precision in the case of certain biotopes such as moorland, poor grassland, and dunes, bogs, fens, peat-bogs, open heathland.

- The exclusion from grant aid of land improvement schemes involving ecologically rare or valuable wetland biotopes found on common grassland and alpine meadows which come under the hill-farming directive (LFA).

- The exclusion from grant aid for the afforestation of poor grassland as well as for ecologically rare or valuable wetland biotopes.

- The commitment to grant aid to coastal protection projects only if the assurance has been given that, among other factors, areas which are of high ecological value, such as salt grassland or mud-flats guarded by dykes, will be established or developed as replacement biotopes (protected areas).

Overall it can be stated that the responsible authorities are increasingly paying more attention to the needs of the protection of nature and the countryside, including soil protection. For instance, in 1980 the Committee for Land Consolidation (a group composed of the highest responsible authorities for land consolidation from the Federal government and from the Länder) passed recommendations for "land consolidation with nature and countryside protection", based on amendments to the 1976 Land Consolidation Act, which advocated greater consideration of ecological demands. Furthermore, in 1983 the Committee for Land Consolidation and the Committee for Nature and Countryside

Protection and Recreation (a group composed of the highest responsible authorities for nature protection from the Länder) agreed joint recommendations concerning the respective relationships between the regulations laid down in the Land Consolidation Act and those of the federal Nature Protection Act.

The federal government will be considering the ecological results in its annual review of the principles for granting aid to improve the agricultural structure and, if necessary, suggest appropriate changes which will, however, need the approval of the Länder.

Protection of the soil and vegetation against harmful substances of non-agricultural origin

Agricultural production is also harmed by substances emanating from non-agricultural activities, from the air, from domestic waste (sewage sludge, refuse tips) and from water (e.g. by floods).

Among these substances, the heavy metals and persistent chemicals (e.g. organochlorines) pose a particular problem, because they form an irreversible accumulation in the soil. This can cause considerable imbalance in microbiological processes and lead to contamination of agricultural products, which affects the quality of the foodstuffs. The accumulation of these substances in the soil has been considered a local and partly a regional problem until now: areas in the vicinity of industrial sites with their harmful emissions, areas which were regularly fertilised with sewage sludge, areas which were often flooded. In these cases measures have been taken in the last 10 years with the help of the water supply law, the waste water charging law, the federal emission control law, the waste disposal law and the sewage sludge regulations, with the result that spectacular cases of accumulations of dangerous substances in agriculturally-used soils are now rare. These regulations will at least guarantee a decrease in soil-contamination in future.

However, it has been established recently that apart from noxious gases such as sulphur dioxide, heavy metals, too, are transported over long distances. For example, cadmium emissions from industrial plant have been measured in far distant areas, in quantities of 10 to 20 g per hectare per year, whereas the natural loss through plant production and leaching into deeper soil strata was only 5 g per hectare and per year. According to our present knowledge, this phenomenon can be explained largely by the fact that industries responsible for harmful emissions have fulfilled their legal obligations as regards the protection of human health, but also as regards the protection of soils and vegetation in their immediate vicinity by building high chimneys. To counter the long-distance transport of dangerous emissions, the so-called regulation for large scale incinerators was established in 1983, and a more stringent regulation on clean air (TA Luft)* for smaller industrial plants is in preparation. Both regulations aim at a drastic reduction of emissions by setting limiting standards for their sources. These measures are also useful to combat locally or regionally existing toxic effects of air emissions (e.g. from SO_2, F, and their derivations and ozone) which are responsible for decreasing yields and damage to agricultural cultivation.

Time is too short for me to elaborate on the even greater importance of these measures for the protection of our forests.

The implementation of existing law by the administration and the courts

To implement the federal law the Länder have often enacted instructing regulations for their administration which give detailed advice on their legal handling. This is the case, for example, for the regulation on sewage sludge.

The implementation of those regulations in the service of nature and health protection, which demand a licensing of substances before they may be used for agricultural purposes (pesticides, fertilisers, veterinary pharmaceuticals) presents no problems. These substances cannot be marketed without a licence. Furthermore there are strict controls for the sale of licensed but dangerous substances. This is not so much the case as regards the handling of these substances once they are in the hands of the farmer, because controls are much more difficult to impose, due to the large number of farm enterprises involved.

_____
* TA Luft = Technische Anleitung zur Reinhaltung der Luft = general administrative regulation on clean air.

Problems with implementation sometimes exist on a regional basis in the vicinity of the borders where farmers buy pharmaceuticals, which are not licensed or are prohibited in our country, in the neighbouring country because they are cheap. The number of these cases has decreased, however, thanks to strict legal prosecutions.

In general, implementation also presents few problems where legally based (grant) aids for the benefit of environmental protection have been linked to certain conditions. Here, it can be seen from the plans, which have to be submitted to the responsible authorities in advance, whether or not these conditions (for instance, prohibition on draining moorland) are being fulfilled.

Consistent implementation is more difficult, if regulations concerning the application of certain substances exist for reasons of environmental protection (for example, use of sewage sludge in agriculture, use of fertiliser in water protection zones and in the near future the limited use of pesticides). In these cases problems can arise from the sheer number of farms, the limited personnel and technical equipment available to the authorities, and also from the organisational separation of legal competence and technical knowledge in the implementing authorities at the lower end of the scale, and, finally, from the lack of experience in the implementing of new regulations. As a result of increasing experience and the availability of more highly-qualified personnel to the authorities, and also better cooperation between the authorities, implementation of the regulations has already improved recently even in this area.

Sanctions which are available to the administration or the Courts are, as far as I know, few in number, and consist of compensatory payments, fines, prosecutions, relevant sentences. There are several reasons for this: the awareness of the problem has increased among farmers in recent years due to systematic training and the use of advisory services, so that spectacular cases of environmental pollution have become rarer. Strong criticism voiced by the public recently in matters of infringements of the environmental legislation has also played an important part, but also, of course, over the limited possibilities for control. Furthermore sanctions in individual cases which have been widely publicised in the national and agricultural press have deterred many farmers.

Finally the small number of sanctions can be attributed to the extraordinary difficulties for the authorities to prove the guilt of farmers. Noxious substances can often be found in non-agricultural emissions or are a natural component of the soil. If penalties or fines are inflicted, they are usually relatively low, and rarely exhaust all legal possibilities. This obviously cannot be seen as a deficiency, because in the official view it is not the extent of the penalty inflicted but the fact that it was inflicted which achieves the change in attitude to be desired.

How could the administration make even more progress in the implementation of environmental legislation?

Firstly, progress can be made by minimising the problems of implementation indicated above:

- better provision of manpower as regards numbers and qualifications, together with technical equipment for the authorities.

- further education of personnel.

- better cooperation between the responsible authorities (police, agricultural and water authorities).

- better cooperation between the administration and the farmers (which is just as important) so that infringements of the law can be avoided; a stronger emphasis on environmental needs in education; further education and advisory services should be the aim, since preventive activities are more effective than penalties or than the elimination of acute dangers and damage.

- promotion of agricultural activities which diminish the risk for
  the environment, for instance: financial aids for the
  construction of adequate storage capacity for slurry so that
  spreading in winter can be avoided.

- promotion of research projects for the minimisation of noxious
  emissions to the soil and for the improvement of species and
  biotope protection: the aim here would be to make legal
  environmental protection more effective by rapid adaptation to
  scientific knowledge.

The application of the "polluter-pays" principle for agriculture

This principle, which demands monetary compensation for damage
to the environment by the polluter, is - in my view - only applicable to
agriculture on a limited scale. Let me illustrate my opinion with two
examples: heavy metal residues or residues of dangerous organic
substances in agricultural products usually do not only result from
fertilising with, for example, cadmium-rich phosphates, sewage sludge or
from the use of pesticides. Heavy metals are also - as already
mentioned - a natural component of the soil and accumulate on
agricultural surfaces and cultivations as a result of industrial
emissions. The agents responsible for pollution in these cases are
nature, agriculture, industry and transport, and it is not possible to
calculate their exact shares in the result. The same can be said for
ground water contamination with nitrate. This should not lead us to the
conclusion that agriculture should be allowed to continue to contribute
its share in the irresponsible pollution of the countryside. On the
contrary, it has to make every effort to minimise its damaging impact
upon the environment. What should be done has already been pointed out.

Codes of good practice - how effective are they?
What is the opinion of farmers' organisations concerning these codes?

The codes of good practice as a means to solving problems is the
preferred instrument in Anglo-American legal thinking. Insofar as they
are agreements between the authorities and farmers for the protection or

restoration of certain environmental features by certain types of farm management, there is nothing comparable in West Germany, as far as I know.

But since agricultural training and advisory services have now started to pay increased attention to environmental problems, a lot of publications have been issued in recent years with recommendations for the achievement of an agricultural production system which is beneficial to the environment. These have, of course, no legal force. These publications which are widely read in the farming community give practical hints on, for example, how to eliminate excessive odours in animal production, how to use fertiliser economically and (ecologically) correctly, how to apply pesticides or how to decrease ground water contamination with nitrate by using certain methods of cultivation. These publications are in special demand from younger farmers. My impression is that these farmers have the strongest motivation for environmental protection, which could be a result of the increased emphasis placed upon environmental problems during their education.

The agricultural organisations welcome informal recommendations. Furthermore they themselves organise numerous seminars on the topic of environmental protection and agriculture with considerable cooperation from the administration. The interest of farmers in these seminars is increasing. This is especially true of meetings which discuss ways for a possible synthesis of ecology and economy. I think that the farmers are willing to cooperate with the authorities. The more qualified and balanced the advice that is given, the more willing is the farmer to accept that advice. A purposeful extension of the advisory service is therefore an important contribution to the more effective implementation of environmental legislation, and hence to an increased regard for the environment in agriculture. This judgment should not however (from the German point of view) direct one to the misleading conclusion that an improved advisory service in combination with better training and education of the farmer could make environmental legislation superfluous.

"Agriculture, especially modern technical-chemical agriculture, has made considerable changes in the harmony of the natural economy - though it is itself dependent upon it - and has, in particular, impaired nature's self organisation and self regulation, and has even partially destroyed it.

"This represents a crucial intervention in the ecological balance, which can be neither avoided nor reversed, because it would mean the renunciation of all agricultural activity. It must be accepted that the very use of land for systematic cultivation is a form of use to which nature is averse, but also for the sake of agriculture itself nothing should remain untried to prevent and decrease harmful effects upon the ecological balance." (Prof. Haber)

If these harmful effects are to be prevented, decreased or compensated effectively, it is necessary to direct the further development of the agricultural system in such a way that the natural limits of the environment are not violated or even transgressed. To achieve this aim, formal legal regulations are necessary as well as the other measures discussed earlier in this paper.

A sympathetic but sober advocate for environmental protection, who is no particular friend of the reputedly exaggerated German sense of the importance of law and order, has put forward this very realistic (to my way of thinking) argument:

"It is not what scientists discuss, citizens demand, lobbies attack and politicians say that creates obligations, even though many such contributions may serve as guides for future developments. It is only the legal position and its implementation that brings about action on behalf of the environment. Therefore the legislation is a strong pillar in the support of the whole sphere of environmental protection."

THE EFFECTIVENESS OF ENVIRONMENTAL LEGISLATION
The de facto situation in the EEC

Hubert V. David
European Environmental Bureau, Brussels

Summary

The European Environmental Bureau (EEB) is a liaison body for sixty leading environmental organisations from every Member State in the European Community. The EEB itself and its member bodies have been very much concerned with environmental policy as well as with agricultural policy. Under the Common Agricultural Policy, both the price support system which favours intensive farming and the structural policy which funds the destruction of wildlife and countryside features have been the subject of EEB interventions.

May I mention here that this paper is presented in my personal capacity only. I should like also to make a preliminary remark on some of the roots of conflict between the environment and agriculture in recent years. In my opinion, these conflicts arise to a large extent from the price policy of the CAP. It has become profitable to use marginal land and intensive inputs, and thus more and more habitats have become endangered, or have disappeared.

Institutional problems

The fragmentation of legislative work is a major problem for making the environmental policy effective. Pesticides are decided upon by the Agricultural Council, and so is the forestry policy, taking only two examples related to agriculture. The Third Action Programme on the Environment, adopted on 7 February last year, clearly stipulates that all Community policies must take into account their impact upon the environment; whether or not this will prove effective has still to be seen. The present reform of the Agricultural Structures Directives is, for the EEB, the test-case.

There are a large number of Community policies affecting both the environment and agriculture which are neglected to some extent by the farmers and the environmentalists' lobby. Yet these are of major importance for the introduction of a comprehensive environmental policy as applied to the agricultural sector. Regional policy is a major example. But, taking another example, the Community's social policy should not be overlooked. If one is to achieve a good social policy for the lower income farmers the pressure to increase agricultural prices every year should be removed, thus stopping the spiral towards more intensive farming and environmental destruction.

The reason why a comprehensive package never emerges is mainly due to the fragmented legislative process as described above.

Participation by interests other than strictly short-term economic interests is poor at Community level. Farmers' organisations are well represented in the Community's official participation machinery, namely the Economic and Social Committee. Environmentalists who represent many more Community citizens are not represented. Yet, the Royal Society for the Protection of Birds (UK) alone has more members than the combined membership of the National Farmers' Union and the Country Landowners' Association. Issues are being discussed and advice given at the ESC meetings which matter as much to the RSPB member as to the NFU and the CLA. In its present composition, the ECS is, as far as environmentalists are concerned, virtually useless.

The European Investment Bank is an institution of the European Community which is often forgotten. In the past, it has financed large-scale agricultural projects, promoting intensive, and thus environmentally harmful, agriculture.

The resolution of the Environment Ministers on the Third Action Programme is, in principle, binding on the Bank as well as its Board (the Ministers of Finance). Management, at least in theory, should from now on consider the environmental impact of loans to agricultural projects and refuse loans in cases of danger for the environment. Many people are no doubt anxious to see if this will come about.

The Bank's senior officials claim that over the past few years, and before the Resolution of the Council of Ministers in February 1983, they were already studying the environmental impact of all loan projects.

Finally, the unanimity rule in the Council of Ministers is a major obstacle to the introduction of a daring, progressive environmental policy. Certainly, the unanimity rule has prevented some environmentally destructive proposals from being passed (for example, the heavy lorry proposals and others), but on balance it is a negative element. The Commission cannot draft any far-reaching proposals in matters of pollution control (air, water, etc.), while the Council of Ministers takes every proposal down to its lowest possible common element.

Implementation

Directives form binding legislation for the Member-States' legislature or regulatory institutions. Yet, the very secrecy of the meetings of the Council of Ministers makes control by public opinion, Press and national Parliaments impossible. The only published paper is the actual law, the Directive. Ministers often have their remarks or reserves noted in the minutes of the Council meeting; these remarks obviously indicate how a particular Minister intends to implement the Directive in his own country. And yet these minutes are secret.

Directives and regulations have to be implemented by the Member States, no matter what may be the opinions of the national Parliaments. Depending on the support of his national and powerful interests groups, a Minister can speed up or slow down the implementation of any agreement. Also, one should not underestimate the sometimes genuine problems in implementing environmental legislation due to lack of staff. Often the division of power between the national government (which negotiates in Brussels) and the regional governments or counties is also a problem.

None of the Member States can claim that it has implemented all environmental Directives on time. Officially, Member States can be taken to the European Court for non-implementation. Some have in fact been taken to the Court, for instance Belgium, for non-compliance on anti-pollution Directives and France on the Birds Directive.

But the process has a great deal of inbuilt "disincentive". A Member State will not take its fellow Member State to the Court for non-implementation as long as itself is not fully implementing all the Directives and Regulations. The Commission is constantly negotiating with all Member States on the drafting of new proposals for Directives and feels that filing a complaint against a Member State might weaken its good negotiating climate with that particular Member State.

Environmental policies

Most of the above problems are not specifically related to the environmental sector; they are emerging in many fields. In the second part I would like to outline some of the problems specifically related to environmental issues.

It has been said many times, not least in the UK, that the lack of a specific article in the Treaty of Rome on which to base the environment policy is a major impediment. Although I would not go so far as to say that a specific article would not have made matters much easier, personally I do not attach a great deal of importance to the absence of such an article. In fact, there have been many proposals and some agreements in environmental sectors which are not covered at all by the Treaty; for example, the initial opposition by the Federal Republic of Germany and by Denmark against the Birds Directive on the grounds of the lack of legal basis quickly disappeared when there was a clear political will in those countries to pass the Birds Directive.

The lack of specific reference to environment in the Treaty forces the Environment Council to make decisions unanimously. But even for those matters specifically mentioned in the Treaty, the Council now rules by unanimity in any case since the "Luxembourg" compromise, so that in practice it does not make any difference.

Political will is the main asset lacking for a daring, comprehensive European environmental policy. A few examples of the present situation are given below;

- the stubbornness of the United Kingdom in continuing with its traditional quality standards approach;
- the opposition of the Danish Parliament to a compulsory Environmental Impact Statement procedure;
- the reluctance shown by many Member States to tackle the long-range transboundary air pollution.

It is also relevant to mention that, as yet, environment has been on the agenda only three times at Summit meetings:

- in 1972 to start the environmental programmes;
- in 1978 to react to the Amoco Cadiz accident;
- in 1983 to discuss acid rain and lead in petrol.

Nevertheless, public interest and support for the environmental cause remains very high.

There are severe budgetary and staffing constraints at Commission level. The budget for environment at the Commission in 1983 was only 9,450,000 ECU (or roughly over 5,000,000 pounds sterling). In 1983 only sixty-six persons were on the staff of the Environment Directorate of the European Commission. This staff is furthermore overburdened with routine activities such as reporting to the Council and its working groups so that the conception and promotion of an environmental policy, as well as the monitoring of its implementation by the Member States, is continually being delayed.

Finally, it should not be forgotten that the behaviour of national scientific and administrative establishments has not helped to speed up a smooth and rapid implementation of Community environmental policy. Neither should it be forgotten that scientific debate is on-going, and that some politicians take this debate as an alibi for slowing down imnplementation.

Conclusion

I realise that many questions asked by the organisers are not answered. The reason is that I do not have the answers. The above outline only tries to picture the general context of the de facto implementation of the Community's environmental policy.

SESSION III

ASSESSING THE COST OF ENVIRONMENTAL LEGISLATION TO THE FARMER

N.T. Williams

Farm Business Unit, Wye College (University of London)

Introduction

The purpose of this paper is to examine the possible impact of environmental protection measures on farm incomes in the United Kingdom. Measures involving restrictions on polluting activities as well as charging purification costs to the industry will be discussed. However, the sheer scale and complexity of the area to be considered means that not all potentially polluting farming activities can be examined. Instead, attention has been directed towards some of the most topical issues – nitrate levels in water and straw burning. Attention is also briefly directed to situations where greater environmental awareness could lead to direct financial benefit to farmers.

Methodological problems

The debate on the environmental impact of agricultural practices has led to many suggestions for changes to existing legislation, for example, the banning of straw burning. Such uncertainty about possible new legislation and the difficulty of enforcing existing legislation because of the non-point source of much pollution emanating from agriculture makes any estimate of the cost of environmental legislation to the farmer difficult and highly dependent on the underlying assumptions regarding the standards set by the legislation. The decision on the level of standards that should apply is itself a complex one as many of the costs of pollution are difficult if not impossible to quantify in economic terms. Any assessment of the costs of environmental pollution must involve a high level of subjective judgment by the legislative body if a decision on the optimum balance between agriculture and society as a whole is to be achieved.

If this balance can be identified then the polluting activities can be taxed in such a way that the external costs of pollution are internalised to the polluter, thereby causing him to reduce his level of pollution in response to economic forces. In the absence of such information or consensus on the social optimum, it may only be possible to identify the cost of reducing the level of pollution to an acceptable level, for example, in the treatment of drinking water, and charge this to the polluters by means of a levy or tax linked to their use of the pollutant.

Unfortunately, the possible effect of environmental legislation on agricultural incomes is not easy to measure. The internalisation of the costs of pollution via taxes would reduce income directly because of the additional costs involved, but would also probably lead to a lower level of intensity within some enterprises and also to a change in the mix of enterprises. These changes would be constrained because farmers vary in their ability to alter enterprise mixes due to differences in physical factors and the quantity and quality of land available to them, climatic conditions and proximity to markets as well as to differences in capital availability and managerial skills.

Changes in levels of output could be expected to lead to changes in product prices and therefore in profitability of the different enterprises which would in turn lead to further adjustments. These price changes would depend on the elasticities of demand for the product, and on other factors such as the effect of the Common Agricultural Policy. In the latter case a fall in production of a commodity need not lead to an increase in its price if there is a structural surplus of that commodity which is greater than the fall in production. Although there would be a saving in community funds required to finance any reduced surplus which would be of benefit to society as a whole, it is doubtful whether, in the current economic and political climate, much of this would be allowed to accrue to farmers through increased price support.

Any fall in demand for inputs could be expected to lead to a reduction in the price demanded by the suppliers. This again could lead to a change in relative profitabilities of different enterprises and an increase in the use of the input from its ideal level.

A further complicating factor is that within the EEC, while each country has an obligation to achieve certain environmental standards, such as water quality, the individual countries are at liberty to choose their own methods of achieving the standards. If some countries chose to achieve the required standards by using public rather than farmers' funds, then there would be a distortion of competition between countries which would be detrimental to the incomes of farmers in those countries where the costs of controlling pollution are internalised to the industry.

All these factors make it extremely difficult to predict the effect of present and proposed environmental legislation on agriculture without the use of sophisticated econometric models. Some attempts have been made to do this with certain pollutants (Turner, Hartley), but the practical applicability of the pollution control methods modelled may be open to doubt because of their complexity.

While it is beyond the scope of this paper to make a detailed econometric analysis of such legislation, it is possible to examine the sensitivity of margins and profits to various legislative measures that have been proposed to regulate some of the more important sources of pollution.

Nitrates

The EEC Directive on quality of water for human consumption states that the maximum acceptable concentration of nitrate in water should be 50 mg/litre. It recommends a guide level of 25 mg/litre. The Directive has caused concern because many rivers in the South East and Midlands intermittently exceed the maximum permissible level.

If the Directive's limits are not to be exceeded, the levels of nitrate have to be reduced either by treatment to extract nitrates or by reducing the quantity of nitrate entering the water system.

Nitrogenous fertiliser and animal excretion are two of the main sources of nitrates in the water system through surface run-off and leaching. Any attempt to reduce nitrate pollution of water would involve reducing application of these commodities to agricultural land. This can be achieved by either setting legislative constraints or by raising the price of the input through taxes.

Nitrogenous fertiliser

The neo-classical theory of production assumes that, over the relevant range, each additional unit of input produces a lower level of output than the preceding unit of input. This is known as the Law of Diminishing Marginal Returns. Given constant prices, the profit maximising entrepreneur will increase his use of the input until the value of the output from a unit of the input is equated to the price per unit of that input.

If the price of a unit of input falls (or the value of output rises) then production will be increased as more input is used until a new equilibrium is reached. Conversely, if the price of a unit of input is increased then the entrepreneur will reduce his use of the input. A tax on nitrogenous fertiliser would raise the price per unit of that fertiliser and therefore should reduce its use according to this theory.

However, a considerable body of evidence exists that indicates that the response of many temperate crops to nitrogenous fertiliser is linear or made up of linear segments (Cooke, Eagle et al.). Up to a certain level of input the response per unit of input is constant. Beyond that point further applications will not significantly increase yield if they have any effect at all. Eventually a point will be reached where yield declines.

Given a linear relationship between yield and nitrogenous fertiliser, the rational farmer has only two choices: use that level of fertiliser that generates maximum yield if the price per unit of fertiliser is less than the value of its marginal product, or use no fertiliser if its price is greater than the value of its marginal product.

Table 1. Tax required to induce a reduction in nitrogen application
on different crops

Crop	Av. appl'n of N per ha[1] kg	Av. response per kg N applied[2] kg	Value of product p/kg N p	Cost of kg N p	Tax required per kg to reduce N application p
Winter wheat	166	23	267	33	234
Spring barley	94	15	159	33	126
Maincrop potatoes	199	64	390	33	357

Sources: [1]Church, [2]Royal Commission.

A further complication arises from the fact that different crops
respond at different physical rates to nitrogenous fertiliser
applications. The effect of this is that while a given level of tax
might discourage the use of nitrogen on one crop, it might not lead to
any reduction in application to another crop. Thus some crops would
continue to receive high level applications of a nitrogenous fertiliser
while others would receive none.

Table 2. Effect on yields and outputs of tax-induced reduction
in nitrogen application

Crop	Av. yield per ha (S.E. England)[1] tonnes	Av. output per ha (S.E. England)[1] £	Av. yield per ha with zero kg N[2] tonnes	Av. output per ha with zero kg N £
Winter wheat	6.1	709	2.3	265
Spring barley	4.6	488	3.2	339
Maincrop potatoes	34.4	2104	21.7	1327

Sources: [1]Williams, [2]calculated from response data in Table 1.

There are also considerable variations between regions in a crop's response to nitrogen because of differences in soil type and other factors. This could lead to regional variations in applications of fertiliser to the same crop. Response also varies between seasons and so applications could depend on a farmer's expectations about the probable distribution of favourable and adverse years. These subjective assessments would be difficult to predict.

The relative economic response of different crops to nitrogen depends not only on differences in the physical relationship between the different crops and nitrogen, but also on the relative prices of the products.

If the gross margin of crops to which no nitrogen was applied fell sufficiently because of poorer yields, then there would be a shift away from production of these enterprises into more profitable ones where the value of the marginal product was still greater than the price of nitrogen.

Table 3. Gross output less nitrogen costs per hectare at different levels of tax per kg N

Tax per kg N	p	0	126	234	357
Crop					
Winter wheat	£	654	445	265	265
Spring barley	£	457	339	339	339
Maincrop potatoes	£	2038	1788	1573	1327

Source: Derived from data in Tables 1 and 2.

This shift would have a twofold effect. Firstly, supplies of certain products would increase as more was produced. Logically this should result in a fall in the price of these products and an increase in the price of those products whose production was being discouraged. This might result in a reversal, partial or otherwise, in the change in enterprise mix. Such price changes might, of course, be masked by the effects of the Common Agricultural Policy. If prices did not respond to market forces, then the greater area of crops to which nitrogen was being applied would lead to an increase in total nitrogen applications above the desired level. If prices did respond, then some of the crops to which it has previously been unprofitable to apply nitrogen might once more become sufficiently profitable to justify the use of nitrogen. The extent to which this occurred and the crops for which it occurred would determine what increase, if any, in total nitrogen application above the desired level would take place.

The use of nitrogen quotas is another possible way of reducing the level of nitrate leaching into watercourses. There are two possible methods. The first would involve a flat rate per hectare quota. While simple, this would be distorting. Since more nitrate is leached from arable land than from grassland, a flat rate quota would either overpenalise those producers in the West and North where a greater proportion of the land is under grass and nitrate levels in the water are lower, or allow those in the predominantly arable South and East to use more than the optimum nitrogen, even though nitrate levels in water are already high.

A more efficient system would be to base the quota on each individual farmer's cropping patterns, possibly with allowance made for soil type and other factors that affect leaching of nitrate.

However, recent work by the Agricultural Research Council at Letcombe Laboratory has indicated that a significant proportion of nitrate applied to spring barley as organic fertiliser is transformed into organic matter by soil micro-organisms. This process is not fully understood and must throw doubts on the accuracy of predictions on the rate of loss of nitrogen by leaching.

It seems unlikely that the quota system would involve control over the selection of crops to which the allocated fertiliser would be applied in practice within a farm, if only because of the impossibility of supervising the scheme. It seems likely that the nitrogen would again be allocated to those crops showing the greatest return. Again it would prove difficult to predict the overall effect on enterprise combinations and the resultant product prices.

The size of the necessary nitrate tax and the complexity of the quota system with its suceptibility to abuse would seem to militate against either approach being a practical proposition.

Animal excreta

Similar arguments apply to the control of disposal of animal wastes and the control of nitrogenous fertiliser. In some ways animal wastes might be conceived as being less polluting than nitrogenous fertiliser in that a significant proportion of the constituent nitrogen in them is lost through volatilisation. The Royal Society quotes this as 53 per cent. Against this must be put the fact that much animal waste will be applied to land with the primary purpose of disposing of it rather than using its nutrients. Cost minimising behaviour would lead to it being applied at levels greater than needed for nutritional purposes (Sandiford), with consequent increased pollution per unit applied.

Sandiford has suggested a system of control whereby each farmer has the right to apply animal waste to his land, the quota of waste varying according to animal type, cropping combination, soil type, topography, etc. These quotas would be saleable so that farmers who did not use all their quota could sell the right to spread waste to farmers who have inadequate land to spread all their waste. Anyone with surplus waste would have to dispose of it in some other way or reduce production until the waste produced matched the disposal quota available.

This model would lead to an economically efficient solution and could represent a long-term solution to the problem of disposal of animal wastes. However, it seems likely that, in the short-term at least, the problem of collecting all the necessary data to calculate the quotas and setting up the infrastructure needed to monitor compliance with the scheme could be prohibitively expensive.

Extraction of nitrates

The Royal Society concluded that there is little evidence that recommended levels of nitrogenous fertiliser applications are exceeded. The Control of Pollution Act would not therefore seem the appropriate vehicle for limiting nitrogen applications as there is not a breach of good agricultural practice.

The delays between application of nitrogen and its appearance in water caused by transformation into organic matter and the time taken to percolate through to groundwater suggest that any reductions in nitrogen applications now will not have an immediate pro rata effect on level of nitrates in water.

This indicates that an alternative approach, namely purification, may be necessary. The Royal Society estimated that the cost of reducing nitrate levels in water to an acceptable level over the next 20 years could range between £200 million (Case A) and £1600 million (Case B). Not all of the nitrate in water is due to agricultural practices - much comes from industry and the disposal of domestic sewage. However, it is worth considering the impact on incomes of a decision to charge agriculture the full cost of removing the excess nitrate from water.

As has been discussed, it would be a highly complex task to identify and charge all the sources of nitrate loss from agriculture. An alternative would be to levy a charge on inputs of nitrogen to agriculture.

The Royal Commission suggests that 1,150,000 tonnes of nitrogen are introduced into agriculture each year via fertilisers. A further 1,020,000 tonnes comes from animal wastes. Rainfall and biological N_2 fixation account for a further 425,000 tonnes and a residue of 73,000 tonnes comes from a variety of sources. If the cost of removing excess nitrate from water to render it potable was charged to the sources of nitrogen on a pro rata basis, the following allocation would occur for the assumed minimum and maximum costs, as calculated by the Royal Society.

Table 4. Sources of nitrogen in agriculture and the pro rata allocation of purification charges

Source	Nitrogen tonnes '000[1]	%	Case A £000	Case B £000
Biological N_2 fixation	150	5.6	562	4,498
Seeds	14	0.5	52	420
Fertilisers	1150	43.1	4,310	34,483
Straw	15	0.6	56	450
Silage effluent	9	0.3	34	270
Sewage disposal	26	1.0	98	779
Livestock excreta	1020	38.2	3,823	30,584
Feed waste	9	0.3	34	270
Rain	275	10.3	1,031	8,246
Total	2668	100.0	10,000	80,000

[1] Source: Royal Society.

While it is unlikely that all such costs would justifiably be charged to agriculture, it is of interest to examine the 'worst-case' situation. Deducting the charges accruing to biological N_2 fixation, sewage disposal and rain leaves an annual cost of £8,309,000 and £66,477,000 respectively. The impact of such a charge on agriculture in the UK can be illustrated by the use of the Departmental Net Income Calculation of the Ministry of Agriculture.

Table 5. The effect of a hypothetical nitrate extraction levy
on agriculture

	Case A	Case B
Farming income 1983 (forecast) £million	1536.0	1536.0
Less: Hypothetical annual levy £million	8.3	66.5
Amended farming income £million	1527.7	1469.5
Reduction in farming income %	0.54	4.33
Fertiliser & lime input 1983 (forecast) £million	826	826
Plus: Hypothetical fertiliser levy £million	4.3	34.5
Total fertiliser & lime input £million	830.3	860.5
Increase in fertiliser and lime input %	0.52	4.00
Livestock and livestock products output 1983 (forecast) £million	7062	7062
Less: Hypothetical animal waste levy £million	3.8	30.6
Net livestock & livestock products output £million	7058.2	7031.4
Decrease in livestock & livestock products output %	0.05	0.43

While the effect of such a levy on overall farming income might not appear too onerous at current levels of profitability, it is important to consider the impact of such a levy on the different sectors within the industry.

The largest single levy would be on nitrogenous fertilisers. The increase in overall fertiliser costs caused by the levy is shown in Table 5.

Operation

The operation of the scheme would be relatively simple for nitrogenous fertiliser. A levy of 0.375p per kg nitrogen purchased in Case A or 3p per kg nitrogen purchased in Case B would raise sufficient money to meet the annual cash requirement.

The very low levels of levy would almost certainly not lead to any reduction in application overall or between crops for the reasons discussed earlier. The impact on profitability in different sectors would probably be fairly even, given the remarkably similar average levels of nitrogen application on many major crops (Church).

The levy on animal wastes would be more complex. Data is available on the level of nitrogen in animal excreta (Cooke) and on the numbers of different livestock in the UK (MAFF). Using the two sets of information, it is possible to allocate the levy to different livestock according to their numbers and average nitrogen production per head. The Royal Commission calculated that production was distributed between the main classes of livestock as shown in Table 6.

Table 6. Allocation of hypothetical nitrate extraction levels between
          the different categories of livestock in the UK

Class of livestock	Excretion of N tonnes ('000s)[1]	Levy £000	Levy £000
Cattle and horses	650	2,436	19,490
Sheep and goats	215	806	6,447
Pigs	70	262	2,099
Poultry	85	319	2,548
Total	1,020	3,823	30,584

Source: [1]Royal Society.

Table 7 shows the average increase in variable costs for some important enterprises that would occur if the hypothetical levies were allocated to them on the basis of their nitrogen application and production.

Table 7. The average levy that would be imposed per hectare and
per head given current agricultural practice in the UK

Crop	Average N Application per hectare[1]	Increase in variable cost per hectare £ Case A (0.375p/kg N)	Case B (3p/kg N)
Winter wheat	166	0.62	4.98
Winter barley	145	0.54	4.35
Spring barley	94	0.35	2.82
Oilseed rape	265	0.99	7.95
Maincrop potatoes	199	0.75	5.97
Sugar beet	144	0.54	4.32
2-7 year leys	173	0.65	5.19
Permanent pasture	96	0.36	2.88

Animal	Average N production per head[2] (kg)		
Cow	68	0.26	2.04
Sheep	10	0.04	0.30
Pig	18	0.07	0.54
100 hens	30	0.11	0.90

Sources: [1]Church, [2]Cooke.

Straw burning

Despite the introduction of more stringent model bye-laws by the
Department of the Environment and the raising of the upper limits on
fines for the breaking of such bye-laws, straw burning continues to
cause problems. These include traffic accidents caused by poor
visibility due to smoke, widespread penetration of buildings by soot
smuts, with consequent cleaning costs, and damage to trees, hedgerows,
and verges by fire. If the bye-laws are observed by farms and if any
breaches of the bye-laws are punished with sufficient severity and
certainty, then the first and third of the above problems should be
greatly diminished.

Much pollution by soot smuts occurs after a field has been burnt unless the ash has been incorporated or is washed into the soil by rain. The present model bye-law states that ash should be incorporated within 36 hours, unless the farmer can show reasonable excuse. This allows sufficient time for much of the ash to be blown off the field and cause pollution. Unless the ash is incorporated on the day of the burn, weather permitting, the smut nuisance will continue and pressure will be maintained for the total abolition of straw burning. Such an abolition could be extremely expensive for agriculture, since some 35 per cent of cereal growers are estimated to burn straw. Straw burning has many advantages and these are briefly listed below.

1. Burning is cheaper than either mechanical incorporation or baling and carting (even after allowing for the sale value of the straw). If burning were to be banned the supply of straw on the market could increase, which would lead to a fall in price and make removal even more unattractive. 75 per cent of straw burnt is wheat straw which has a lower value than barley or oat straw.

2. Burning is the fastest method of clearing straw. This prevents delays to the sowing of winter crops. Yule showed that the delaying of sowing beyond early October depressed winter wheat yields by between 0.29 and 0.89 tonnes per hectare.

   Winter oilseed rape sown in late September or early October always had lower oil content and usually lower seed yield than rape sown in early September (Bowerman and Rogers-Lewis).

3. Cultivating tackle and drills commonly used in the UK often clog up if used on fields where the straw has not been removed. Design changes can remedy this, but unless such machines are bought as part of the normal replacement cycle, which can be very long particularly for ploughs and harrows, this will impose an additional cost on farmers. Currently less than 2 per cent of the straw crop is incorporated.

4. Incorporated straw can reduce yields of the following crops because of:

a)   competition for oxygen from fungi on decomposing straw

b)   immobilisation of nitrogen by the straw during decomposition

c)   production of fatty acids by soil micro-organisms during degradation of straw which reduces the germination rate of seeds and rate of root growth

d)   the creation of an undecomposed layer of vegetable matter in wet clay soils that hinders root penetration and encourages waterlogging.

5.   Burning reduces pest levels, particularly slugs.

6.   Burning can reduce weed populations by destroying both existing plants and ungerminated seed.

Thus although there may be long-term improvements to the soil stemming from incorporation and the reduction in yields can be countered by greater use of nitrogen fertiliser and chemical seed dressing, the case for the abolition of straw burning is not clear cut.

Pesticides

The Code of Good Agricultural Practice, Control of Pollution Act, 1974, states that pesticides "should be used solely for the purposes for which they have been cleared by the Government and limited to the minimum consistent with achieving the desired effects". The Royal Commission on Environmental Pollution identified three possible causes for excessive use of pesticides:

i)   Incorrect perception - farmers may over-estimate the possible losses due to pest attack and also may over-estimate the effectiveness of pesticide application in reducing losses from pest attack.

ii)   Insurance use - the use of a pesticide at a particular time without establishing whether a pest is, in fact, present.

iii) Cosmetic use - the excessive use of a pesticide to improve the appearance of a crop over and above a generally accepted level.

All three causes lead to breaches of the Code of Practice. Even when none of these factors is evident, excessive use may occur because of inadequate machinery or human error. Technological developments such as ultra low volume spraying and controlled droplet application should improve the efficiency of pesticide application and in the process reduce spray costs to the farmer. The Royal Commission assumed that this could lead to a reduction of up to 25 per cent in the total quantity of active ingredient used for the pesticides concerned. The gains to the farmer include reduced purchases of pesticide and less damage to soil structure from lighter equipment or less frequent replenishing of spray tanks. Human error will always be with us.

The problem of over-application, irrespective of which of the three causes it is due to, can best be tackled by education. Considerable work has been carried out on the relationship between environmental factors and subsequent disease levels, for example, Cook and Webster. Computer based models such as the Dutch EPIPRE system have been developed to help in deciding whether or not it is financially worthwhile to spray. Even though such models, or indeed advisory officers, are not perfect, Webster has demonstrated that imperfect information on whether or not to spray can lead to fewer applications of pesticide and greater margins than no information. The balance has then to be struck between the cost of obtaining the information and the saving from reduced applications.

Finally, integrated pest management of cereals using mixtures of resistant and semi-resistant varieties offers a means of reducing the susceptibility of the crop to pest attack while prolonging the useful life of varieties by preventing the build-up of phenotypes of pathogen specific to that variety. Wolfe reports that conventional fungicide treatment of variety mixtures of barley and wheat is generally uneconomic because of the low level of attack.

Some benefits of conservation legislation

Many actions that farmers should take to comply with environmental legislation should not impose a cost on them and may even improve their financial position. As has been noted already, a more conservation-conscious approach to the use of pesticides can increase margins.

The prevention of surface water run-off entering slurry lagoons may result in an initial capital cost for extra drains. However, if this is done the lagoon will require emptying less frequently and the farmer will save on transport and spreading costs in addition to being less likely to suffer an overflow from the lagoon, which could result in a prosecution if pollution of a watercourse occurred.

Experiments are taking place to investigate the value of silage effluent as a feed additive to straw rather than treating it as a highly polluting waste.

The Wildlife and Countryside Act, 1981, S.30(2) states that the Nature Conservancy Council will compensate farmers for any loss in value of their interest in the land to which an order restricting operations is made under Section 29 of the Act.

Other benefits will accrue as new technology becomes available. Anaerobic digestion provides an alternative to land disposal of animal wastes from intensive livestock units. The methane produced as a by-product of this process can be used to produce heat and light for the livestock unit. Widespread adoption of this technique will depend on the availability of reliable, low maintenance units and the price of purchased energy.

Straw may become another useful source of fuel for heating farmhouses, glasshouses, etc. The advent of high density balers will reduce storage and handling problems, but the high capital cost probably means that it will not be economic to replace conventional systems unless they are obsolete.

Conclusions

Pollution caused by agricultural operations is difficult to measure and even harder to control in an equitable manner. The reduction of nitrate levels in water via legislation requires a determined Government in the absence of public pressure and the possibility of derogation of EEC legislation. Even then, all that may be attainable is the treatment of polluted water rather than the prevention of the pollution.

There does appear to be scope for reducing pollution by improved technology and better dissemination of research findings. This applies to the use of nitrogenous fertilisers, for instance, the greater plant uptake from split dressings of nitrogen and the use of 'T sums' to determine when plants will start to respond to nitrogen in the spring, as well as to pesticides.

Finally, the Government should examine the costs and benefits of a grant aid system that subsidised investment in pollution reducing technology such as slurry digesters rather than pollution increasing technology such as field drainage.

References

Bowerman, P. and Rogers-Lewis, D.S. (1980). Effect of Sowing Data on the Yield of Winter Oilseed Rape. Experimental Husbandry, No.36, 1-8.

Church, B.M. (1983). Use of Fertilisers in England and Wales, 1982. Rothamsted Experimental Station Report for 1982, Part 2, 161-168.

Cook, R.J. and Webster, J.P.G. (1977). A Procedure for Making Recommendations for Spraying Winter Wheat against Septoria. Proceedings of 1977 British Crop Protection Conference - Pests and Diseases, 43-48.

Cooke, G.W. (1976). A Review of the Effects of Agriculture on the Chemical Composition and Quality of Surface and Underground Waters. In: Agriculture and Water Quality (MAFF Tech. Bull., No.32), 5-57, London: HMSO.

Control of Pollution Act, 1974, London: HMSO.

Eagle, D.J., Russell, R.D., Boyd, D.A. & Draycott, A.P. (1976). Using Response Curves to Estimate the Effect on Crop Yield and Profitability of Possible Changes in Fertiliser Recommendations. In: Agriculture and Water Quality (MAFF Tech. Bull., No.32), 355-370, London: HMSO.

Hartley, A.G. (1983). An Analysis of Alternative Policies of Nitrogen Control. Unpublished M.A.(Econ) Thesis, Manchester University.

MAFF (1983). Annual Review of Agriculture, 1983 (Cmnd 9137), London: HMSO.

MAFF (1984). Draft Code of Good Agricultural Practice, Control of Pollution Act, 1974.

Royal Commission on Environmental Pollution (1979). Agriculture and Pollution, Seventh Report (Cmnd 7644), London: HMSO.

Royal Society (1983). The Nitrogen Cycle of the United Kingdom. London: The Royal Society.

Sandiford, F. (1984). Controlling Water Pollution from Animal Wastes: A Reconsideration of Economic and Legislative Approaches. Agriculture, Ecosystems and the Environment (in press).

Turner, F. (1979). Economic and Environment Aspects of Animal Waste Management. Unpublished M.A.(Econ) Dissertation, University of Manchester.

Webster, J.P.G. (1982). Value of Information in Crop Protection Decision Making. Proceedings, 1982 British Crop Protection Symposium, 33-41.

Wolfe, M.S. (1981). Integrated Use of Fungicides and Host Resistance for Stable Disease Control. Phil. Trans. R. Soc. Lond. B295, 175-184.

Williams, N.T. (1984). Farm Business Statistics for South East England. Supplement for 1984. Wye College (University of London).

Yule, A.H. (1980). Time of Sowing Winter Wheat on Black Fen Soils. Experimental Husbandry, No.36, 16-19.

ASSESSING THE COST OF ENVIRONMENTAL LEGISLATION TO THE FARMER
IN THE FEDERAL REPUBLIC OF GERMANY

Dr Ernst Berg

Department of Farm Management, University of Bonn

In the past, agricultural production has long been represented as
being in perfect accordance with the objectives of preserving the
quality of the environment and the amenity of the landscape. However,
modern production practices have changed this picture considerably.
Mechanisation and the use of fertiliser and pesticides have reduced the
number of crops in rotation and thus created a rather uniform countryside. Moreover, many people fear that the extensive use of chemicals
might have impacts on the quality of the products as well as on the
quality of water and soil.

Similar developments have taken place in the field of animal
production. Comparative advantages and economies of size have caused a
strong regional concentration of livestock, which in turn has resulted
in considerable problems with respect to manure handling and effluent
odours. In addition, some practices of large scale livestock
production, for example, battery cages, are in conflict with the
objectives of animal protection.

In summary, doubts have been raised that modern farming is
beneficial for the environment. As a consequence, government
regulations have been established and others are under discussion.
These regulations are aimed at benefits in terms of a healthier and more
pleasant environment. At the same time they involve higher production
costs for the farmers. The evaluation of these regulations therefore
requires that both sides, benefits as well as cost, should be taken into
account.

This paper mainly focuses on the latter aspect, the cost of
environmental legislation to the farmer. Drawing upon the situation in
the Federal Republic of Germany, actual legislation as well as possible
future changes will be considered. Because of the differences in the
problems arising, livestock and crop production will be treated

separately. The first part of the paper deals with ecological requirements and their effects upon crop production while the second one refers to the situation in the area of livestock. In the final section some aspects of production allocation and income distribution under the influence of environmental legislation will be outlined.

Economic effects of environmental regulations in crop production

The use of fertiliser and chemical pesticides in agriculture has increased rapidly over the past decades. They have greatly contributed to enhanced agricultural productivity. Given the low rate at which farm land enters the market, increasing the intensity of production has been the only way for many farmers to keep pace with the economic development. However, there is an increasing concern associated with the use of fertiliser and pesticides because of possible residual effects on products, soil and water. Although no pesticide residues in agricultural products have been reported yet, many people are anxious about the existence of problems which are still unrecognised due to a lack of knowledge about the complex effects of these inputs. Some studies report accumulations of plant nutrients, particularly nitrogen, in the ground water (Obermann, 1981).

In addition to these problems, particular groups in the community are concerned with the reduction of biological variability. Simpler rotations and the use of herbicides have decreased the number of plant species found in the countryside. Larger plots and the removal of hedges and ditches at the field boundaries have also contributed to this process.

From this the following problem areas can be defined (Steffen and Schulte, 1982):

- pesticide residues in agricultural products and accumulation of
  plant nutrients in the ground water,
- reduction of the visual complexity of the landscape due to
  simplified production programmes on farms,
- diminishing variability of flora and fauna.

In this paper we shall focus on problems associated with fertiliser and pesticides. Except for areas where ground water is used for drinking purposes no particular regulations with respect to these inputs have as yet been established. However, since there is considerable political pressure it seems worthwhile to evaluate the economic effects of restraints which might be introduced. The effects of reduced fertiliser and pesticide inputs have been investigated in different research projects (Steffen and Berg, 1977; Weinschenck, 1981; Steffen and Schulte, 1982; Schulte, 1983). The following comments relate to those studies.

The model approach

A production function approach was used jointly with linear programming models to calculate the economic effects of nitrogen and pesticide inputs. In general terms a production function can be specified as follows:

$$y = f (x_1 / x_2 \ldots x_n)$$

where y is the output, x_1 the variable input and $x_2 \ldots x_n$ are fixed inputs. In our case x_1 is the amount of nitrogen fertiliser that can be varied continuously. $x_1 \ldots x_n$ represents the other inputs which are either fixed or can be changed only at fixed rates. The latter include chemicals such as growth regulators, herbicides, fungicides and insecticides. Their use provides for a higher potential yield if enough fertiliser is applied. Thus the total production function consists of sets of functions, each of them valid for a particular level of pesticide use. Figure 1 illustrates this conceptual framework using winter wheat as an example. In the figure, the maximum gross margin is achieved at the highest level of pest control with an amount of 160 kg of nitrogen nutrients per hectare (level N_5). Reducing the pesticide level, for instance by omitting the last fungicide spraying, would lead to the next lower part of the production function. The optimal amount of nitrogen would then be at level N_4 (150 kg/ha). The revenue in this case would decrease by 200 DM/ha while the cost saving would only amount to 150 DM/ha, leaving a net loss of 50 DM/ha.

Figure 1. Production function approach for fertiliser
and pesticide application

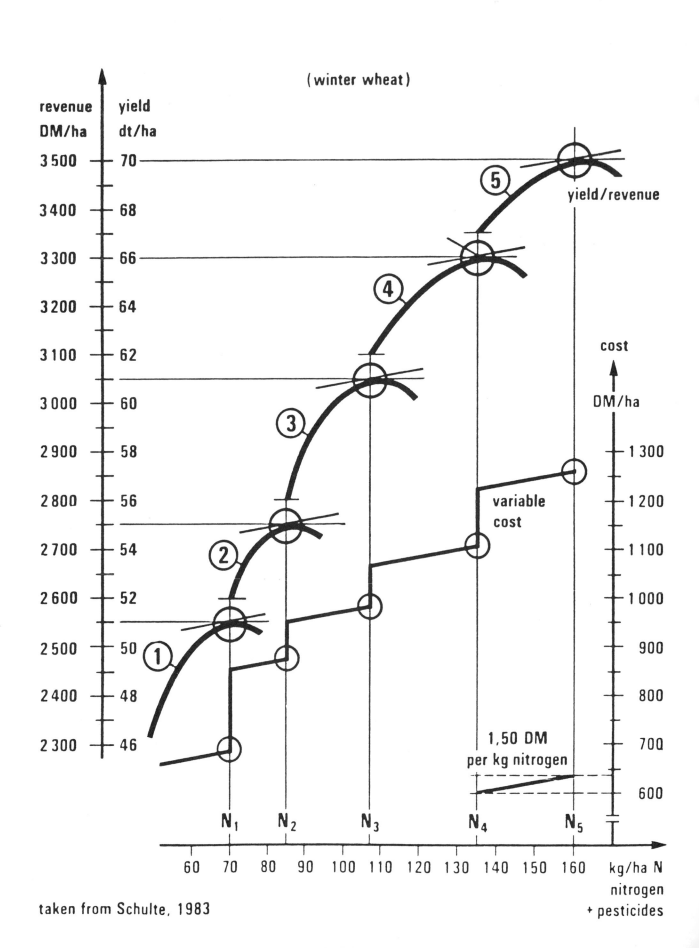

taken from Schulte, 1983

Using this approach along with data from experimental stations and field records of existing farms, linear programming models were formulated for different types of farms at different locations (Schulte, 1983). These models contain a number of production activities for various crops which reflect different levels of production intensity as indicated in Figure 1. The models were then used to investigate the effects of restraints which might be introduced.

Policy options to reduce fertiliser and pesticide levels

If the objective is to reduce fertiliser and pesticide applications in agriculture through government regulations, there are two principal ways in which to accomplish this in the short term (Weinschenck, 1981). The first method is by increasing the respective input prices by means of a tax, while the second is by establishing administrative directives with respect to the use of these inputs. For nitrogen fertiliser for instance a quota system is conceivable that limits the maximum amount per hectare a farmer is entitled to purchase. In the long term, a policy that serves both the needs of farmers as well as consumers would be the support of research work that is directed towards the development of production practices with fewer chemical inputs.

The above models are used as follows to examine the economic effects of input taxation and direct restrictions of fertiliser and pesticide application.

Model results

The economic impacts of conceivable environmental regulations can be illustrated by using two sample farms which are typical for different regions in West Germany:

1. An arable farm without livestock, producing cash crops on an acreage of 100 ha. Yield levels are high (60-70 dt/ha grain yields) and so are the input levels of fertiliser and pesticides. A farm of this nature is fairly typical of the area between Köln and Aachen in the state of Nordrhein-Westfalen.

2. A mixed farming operation with 25 ha of arable land and 5 ha grassland. Yield levels are pretty low (40-50 dt/ha grain yields). Livestock consists of 15 milking cows and 500 fattening pigs. Farms of this type can be found in the state of Hessen.

Table 1 depicts the model results with respect to a tax on nitrogen fertiliser for the first sample farm. It can be seen that a tax of 0.50 DM/kg nitrogen nutrient leads to a reduction of the total nitrogen input by 7%, resulting from a decreased fertiliser application for sugar beet. Higher tax payments further reduce the nitrogen input. If the nitrogen price is increased by 1.50 DM/kg, that is twice the initial price, the total input drops by 15%. At the same time expenditure on fungicide is decreased by 45% due to a lower intensity of wheat production. With a price increase of 2 DM/kg a further reduction of fertiliser and pesticide inputs can be achieved.

However, while the input reduction caused by even relatively high tax payments is quite modest, the effects on net farm income are much more dramatic. A tax rate of 0.50 DM/kg already causes the income to decline by 15%. Higher tax levels lead to profit losses up to 54%.

In the second farm model (Table 2) fertiliser and pesticide inputs react more sensitively to price increases due to taxation. Tax payments of 1.50 DM/kg cause the nitrogen input to decrease by 36%. At a tax rate of 2 DM/kg it even drops to 57% of the initial amount. In this situation the production intensity of all crops is significantly reduced and no more fungicides are applied.

These differences are due to the different yield potentials of the two locations. The second farm operates on a soil of relatively poor quality. In comparison with the former model the slope of the production function is less steep and therefore increasing marginal costs cause a larger input reduction.

The income decline due to taxation is less significant than in the first model. This is due to the fact that a considerable portion of the profit results from livestock, and this remains largely unchanged. However, given the low income level of this farm, even small reductions are crucial for its existence.

Table 3 depicts the effects of administrative directives that limit fertiliser application to a certain amount. The results show that in comparison to the tax system the profit losses are much less dramatic. This is because the input price remains unchanged, so the income decline only amounts to the revenue decrease due to less output minus cost savings due to the input decline. It can be seen that a nitrogen reduction of 10% has hardly any effect on the farm income. Even a 30% reduction of nitrogen together with the associated pesticide decrease leads to a profit loss of not more than 15% in the first model and only 4% in the second one. Turning back to the former results we can see that a similar input effect initiated by taxation would drop the income by more than 50% in the worst case.

Conclusions

These results indicate that, given the actual marginal productivities of nitrogen fertiliser and pesticides, attempts to reduce the application of these inputs via taxation would cause severe income problems for many farms. Cash crop farms in particular would suffer from such regulations. A quota system on the other hand would principally offer the opportunity to reduce the nitrogen and associated pesticide input by a fair amount (for example, 15-20%) without causing severe income losses. However, it is doubtful whether the administrative authorities are able effectively to control such regulations at an acceptable cost level.

With these effects of possible government regulations in mind, farmers are well advised to check carefully whether there are any possibilities for reducing chemical inputs before such regulations are introduced. The advisory services should try to contribute to this process by increasing the farmers' awareness of environmental problems. Also, research work directed towards the development of production practices based on fewer chemical inputs should be given priority. Pest control strategies using economic thresholds as well as fertiliser applications on the basis of control measures of the nitrogen content in plants and soil can lead to a more appropriate production control and fewer environmental problems.

Table 1. Effects of nitrogen taxation - Model 1

		Initial situation	Tax on nitrogen DM/kg			
			0.50	1.00	1.50	2.00
Nitrogen input						
Sugar beet	kg/ha	200	166	160	160	160
Winter wheat	kg/ha	160	160	160	130	130
Winter barley	kg/ha	135	135	135	135	85
Total nitrogen input	kg	16 645	15 538	15 325	14 125	12 775
	%	100	93	92	85	77
Total fungicide	DM	8 089	8 089	8 089	4 489	3 436
expenditure	%	100	100	100	55	42
Net farm income	DM	55 397	47 251	39 498	32 135	25 235
	%	100	85	71	58	46

(Schulte, 1983)

Table 2. Effects of nitrogen taxation - Model 2

		Initial situation	Tax on nitrogen DM/kg			
			0.50	1.00	1.50	2.00
Nitrogen input						
Winter wheat	kg/ha	140	112	112	90	90
Winter barley	kg/ha	130	130	95	95	65
Rye	kg/ha	85	85	85	60	60
Spring barley	kg/ha	85	85	85	60	60
Grassland	kg/ha	250	250	250	150	150
Total nitrogen input	kg	3 400	3 190	2 928	2 165	1 940
	%	100	94	86	64	57
Total fungicide	DM	1 494	976	976	352	-
expenditure	%	100	65	65	24	-
Net farm income	DM	25 639	23 965	22 418	21 193	20 118
	%	100	93	87	83	78

(Schulte, 1983)

Table 3. Effects of limited nitrogen application

		Initial situation	Nitrogen reduction %		
			10	30	50
Model 1					
Grain production	dt	4 690	4 644	4 341	3 878
	%	100	99	93	83
Sugar beet production	dt	16 170	15 510	14 551	13 555
	55	100	96	90	84
Net farm income	DM	55 397	54 392	47 285	30 136
	%	100	98	85	59
Model 2					
Grain production	dt	934	897	859	767
	%	100	96	92	82
Net farm income	DM	25 639	25 455	24 707	23 384
	%	100	99	96	91

(Schulte, 1983)

Economic effects of environmental regulations in animal production

Developments in the livestock area are characterised by a strong regional concentration and a rapid increase in the size of operations. Pollution problems associated with these operations are increasingly becoming a source of friction between farmers and the residents in their neighbourhood. Regulations have therefore been established to cope with the environmental problems associated with large scale livestock operations.

Existing regulations

At present, these regulations are mainly related to pigs and poultry. They are concerned with air pollution (mainly through odour) and the disposal of animal wastes.

As regards the first case, a special directive has been established to evaluate barn arrangements, particularly ventilation systems and manure storage and handling facilities, with respect to odour emissions. A grading scheme ranging from 0 to 100 points is used to categorise the air pollution associated with a particular installation. A minimum score is then required depending on the distance to residential areas. For instance, a 360 head pig operation must score above 80 if located approximately 200 metres from the nearest housing area. The necessary score drops to 15 if the distance is 300 metres. Larger operations require a higher score or a greater distance respectively.

With respect to manure handling the number of animals is related to the acreage available for waste disposal. This can restrict the size of an operation if no more land can be rented or purchased.

Besides these existing regulations there is considerable political pressure to prohibit certain practices in large scale livestock production. At present most attacks are directed towards battery cages for hens, a practice that conflicts severely with the objectives of animal protection.

Economic impacts

The economic impact of environmental regulations with respect to pigs and poultry have been investigated by Schlüter-Craes (1980) and Hinrichs and Kögl (1982). The impact of possible restraints arising from animal protection proposals have been discussed by Hinrichs and Kögl (1982) and Weinschenck and Laun (1983).

The main results of these studies are briefly summarised as
follows:

Regulations with respect to air pollution deal mostly with pig-
fattening operations because of the odour associated with them. In
order to fulfil the requirements, additional investments are necessary.
The resulting economic effects are two-fold. First, the additional
investments increase the cost of production, and secondly they can
affect the growth of the operation. The latter is relevant if capital
is the scarcest resource of the farm, a situation that can be found
fairly often.

In many cases, financial resources put the upper limit on the
amount of capital investments, since banks normally require a certain
portion of the asset to be self-financed.

The direct cost effects associated with investments enforced by
environmental regulations are depicted in Table 4. Three alternatives
are distinguished, relative to the environmental score that is required
at a given distance from the nearest housing area. At the lowest level,
the equipment needed to improve the ventilation of the barn and reduce
the odour from the manure depot (for example by a cover) requires an
additional investment of between 4 and 6 DM per animal, depending on the
size of the operation. If a score of 80 has to be achieved, the
necessary investment ranges from 18 DM for large operations (more than
1000 animals) to 33 DM for smaller ones (for example 300 animals). The
last column of Table 4 represents the maximum reduction of air pollution
that is possible with the available technology. Achieving this standard
requires financial inputs between 31 and 57 DM per unit capacity.

The additional costs of production caused by these investments
range from 1 DM per animal and year in the best cases to more than 16 DM
in the worst ones. Assuming an initial net return of approximately
22 DM per animal and year we obtain the percentage profit reduction as
given in the last row of Table 4. If a high environmental score is
required due to the proximity of housing areas, profits may drop rather

- 88 -

heavily. In such cases it could be reasonable to move the operation
further out in the countryside in order at least partly to avoid the
need for these investments.

Table 4. Economic effects of additional investments
to reduce air pollution

		Additional investment		
		Low	Medium	High
Environmental score		60	75	100
Capital requirement	DM/head	4 - 6	18 - 33	31 - 57
Capital costs (depreciation and interest)	DM/head/year	0.4 - 0.6	2.2 - 4.6	4.9 - 9.8
Operating costs	DM/head/year	0.6	3.2 - 4.0	5.1 - 6.8
Total additional costs	DM/head/year	1.0 - 1.2	5.4 - 8.6	10.0 - 16.6
Profit reduction	%	5 - 6	25 - 39	45 - 75

(Schlüter-Craes, 1981)

If environmental investments restrict the growth of an operation,
the economic impacts will even be stronger. Hinrichs and Kögl (1982,
p.340) for instance report that the present value of the cost associated
with environmental regulations increases by approximately 50 per cent if
the additional capital requirement causes the investment to be delayed
by 5 years.

Since the costs of these environmental regulations depend on the location of an operation relative to residential areas, they have considerable influence on the competition between farms. Differences of only a few hundred metres in the distance from housing areas can cause income differences of several thousand marks (Hinrichs and Kögl, 1982, p.343). Moving the operation further out in the countryside in order to avoid additional investment costs normally causes high development costs. These are justifiable only if the operation exceeds a certain size. Thus regulations of that sort can in fact contribute to a further concentration of livestock.

Many poultry operations are heavily attacked by animal protectionists. Keeping several hens in a cage with very limited space is felt to be cruelty to the animals and therefore a violation of ethical principles. Experiments indicate that in fact a high occupation density of the hen-house results in an increased mortality and lower egg yields (Hinrichs and Kögl, 1982, p.344). However, cost savings - particularly with respect to capital investments and labour input - by far outweigh these disadvantages. So the production methods under attack turn out to be highly profitable, and preventing them would result in a considerable cost increase. Several studies have found that the economic detriment associated with production practices that are more adapted to the natural behaviour of the animals can amount to 6 to 7 DM per hen and year (Hinrichs and Kögl, 1982; Weinschenck and Laun, 1983). A price increase of 2 to 3 Pf per egg, that is 12 to 18 per cent, would be necessary to offset the higher cost.

Market effects of environmental regulations

Environmental legislation does not necessarily affect all farmers equally. For instance, regulations concerning the air pollution of livestock operations affect only those farms that are located fairly close to urban areas. Restrictions with respect to fertiliser application occur mainly in regions where ground water is used for drinking purposes. Also, production restraints in natural reserves apply only to particular groups of farms. In these cases the competition between the farms is affected, so changes in production allocation and income distribution may occur that have to be taken into account.

These effects are largely dependent on the particular market conditions. Figure 2 illustrates the impacts of environmental regulations, using the common one-commodity supply and demand model (Berg and Steffen, 1979). Two groups of producers (i and j) are distinguished, one of which (j) is assumed to be affected by environmental regulations. If no regulations exist, $A_{o,i}$ and $A_{o,j}$ are the respective supply functions of these two groups of farms. A_o then represents the total supply. For a given demand function N the equilibrium price of the commodity is P_o, while the market volume amounts to M_o.

If environmental legislation increases the production costs of group j, the respective supply function will be shifted to the left, indicating a decline of supply if the price remains unchanged. In Figure 2 the new supply function is given by $A_{1,j}$. The total supply then also drops to A_1 resulting in a higher equilibrium price (P_1). This price increase enables the producers of group j to transfer a part of the cost associated with the environmental legislation to the consumers, while only the remaining part results in profit losses. The farmers that are not affected by the regulations (group i) also gain the benefits of the higher price. As a consequence they would increase their production to $M_{1,i}$ and thus earn additional profits due to a higher price and a larger market share. In summary, in this case the environmental regulations would result in a higher market price, a net reduction of the total supply and a shift of the production towards the unaffected group of producers. Furthermore, the latter would gain a net profit from the regulation.

The above situation implies a competitive market, that is administrative price support does not exist, or at least is ineffective. Thus, under European conditions it applies for example to pig or egg production. For commodities where the administrative prices are well above the equilibrium price, for example sugar beet and grain, the effects of environmental regulations are different. At the guaranteed price level P_{int} the total supply (M'_o) exceeds the demand (M_N). The surplus is removed from the market by government

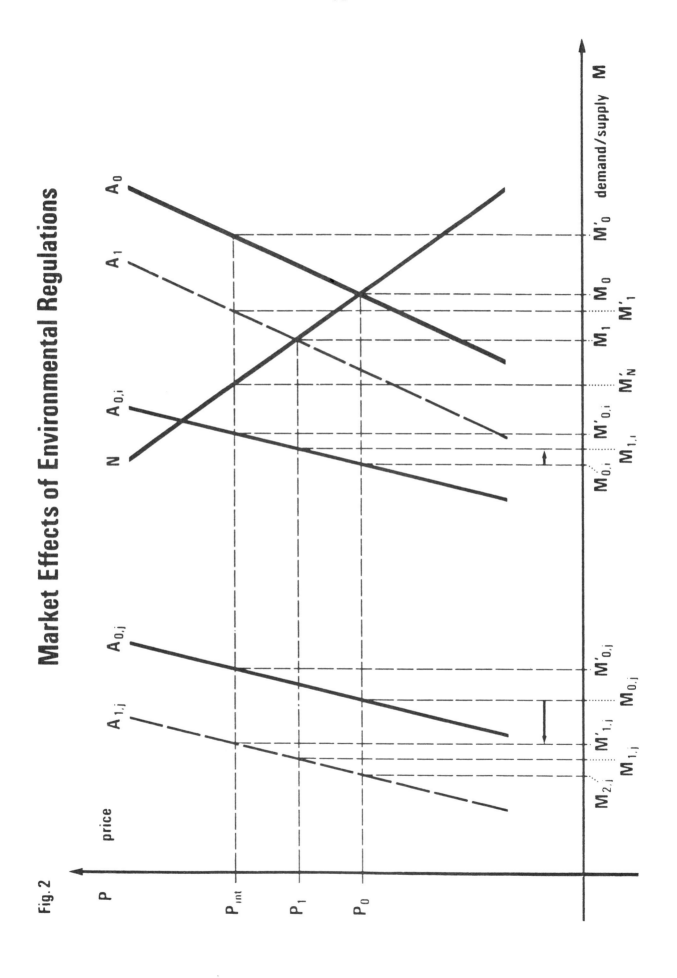

Fig. 2

Market Effects of Environmental Regulations

intervention. If now the production costs of producer group j are increased, the total supply function will be shifted to A_1. This will have no impact on the price level as long as the administrative price remains above that which would occur under conditions of market equilibrium. Consequently, the affected producers have no chance to transfer additional costs to the consumers but must bear the resulting profit losses completely by themselves. For the other farmers the situation remains unchanged. Since the market surplus diminishes, there is a net benefit on the part of the consumers, because of lower costs associated with an inferior utilisation of the excess production. In this situation there is no shift of the production towards producer group i, while the farmers of group j have to bear the total costs of the regulation.

This illustrates the proposition that different effects with respect to production allocation and income distribution may be associated with legislative acts. Politicians should consider these impacts when issuing environmental regulations. Particular thought must be given to the distributional effects as long as the provision of a satisfactory farm income remains a predominant objective of agricultural policy.

Most of the same effects which have been illustrated above for different groups of producers within one country can occur on the level of the European Community. If environmental legislation differs significantly among the EC countries, distortions of competition will occur that result in market effects as indicated above. Particularly on competitive markets (for example the egg market) production would be shifted markedly towards the country with the least significant restraints. Therefore a reasonably uniform legislation is necessary to avoid relative disadvantages to the farmers in individual countries.

References

Berg, E. und Steffen, G., 1979. Agrarproduktion und Umwelt
    - Umweltkonflikte und Ansätze zu ihrer Darstellung und Lösung, in:
    Berichte über Landwirtschaft, Bd. 57, H. 2, S. 210-234.

Hinrichs, P. und Kögl, H., 1982. Ökonomische Auswirkungen von Umwelt-
    und Tierschutzauflagen in der tierischen Veredlungsproduktion, in:
    Landwirtschaft unter veränderten Rahmenbedingungen, Schriften der
    Ges. für Wirtschafts- und Sozialwiss. des Landbaues e.V., Bd. 19,
    Münster-Hiltrup, S. 335-351.

Obermann, P., 1981. Nitratbelastung des Grundwassers im Einzugsgebiet
    von Wasserwerken, in: Landbewirtschaftung und Ökologie, Arbeiten
    der DLG, Bd. 172, S. 39-43.

Schlüter-Craes, F.H., 1981. Ökonomische Auswirkungen von
    Umweltschutzauflagen in Betrieben mit Schweine- und Geflügel-
    haltung, Bonner Hefte für landwirtschaftliche Betriebslehre, H. 6,
    Stuttgart.

Schulte, J., 1983. Einfluss eines begrenzten Handelsdünger- und
    Pflanzenbehandlungsmitteleinsatzes auf Betriebsorganisation und
    Einkommen verschiedener Betriebssysteme, Diss., Bonn.

Steffen, G. und Berg, E., 1977. Einfluss von Begrenzungen beim Einsatz
    von Umweltchemikalien auf den Gewinn landwirtschaftlicher
    Unternehmen, Materialien zur Umweltforschung, hrsg. vom Rate der
    Sachverständigen für Umweltfragen, Wiesbaden.

Steffen, G. und Schulte, H., 1982. Einzelbetriebliche Beurteilung von
    Massnahmen zur Verringerung der Umweltbelastung im Bereich der
    Bodennutzung, in: Vorträge der 35. Hochschultagung der
    Landwirtschaftlichen Fakultät der Universität Bonn am 2. und
    3 März 1982, Münster-Hiltrup, S. 91-107.

Steffen, G. und Schulte, J., 1982. Wirtschaftliche Auswirkungen von
    Umweltschutzauflagen im Bereich der pflanzlichen Produktion, in:
    Landwirtschaft unter veränderten Rahmenbedingungen, Schriften der
    Ges. für Wirtschafts- und Sozialwiss. des landbaues e.V., Bd. 19,
    Münster-Hiltrup, S. 317-333.

Weinschenck, G., 1981. Ökologische Forderungen und ihre Auswirkung auf
    die wirtschaftliche Entwicklung, in: Landbewirtschaftung und
    Ökologie, Arbeiten der DLG, Bd. 172, Frankfurt, S. 140-154.

Weinschenck, G. und Laun, H., 1983. Ethik und Ökonomik des
    Tierschutzes in der landwirtschaftlichen Nutztierhaltung,
    Agrarwirtschaft, Jg. 32, S. 69-76.

SESSION IV

THE EFFECTS OF AN IMPLEMENTATION OF STRICTER LEGISLATION: THE REACTION OF THE CONSUMER

Professor W. Heeschen
Institute for Hygiene, Federal Dairy Research Centre, Kiel

Introduction

The First Environmental Programme of the government of the Federal Republic of Germany was passed on 29 September, 1971. Already at that time one of the targets of this programme was extensively to analyse the present state of the biosphere. Priority was to be given to researches into

- the effects of biocides and environmental chemicals on men, animals and plants and, in addition,
- the detection, control and assessment of the occurrence of biocides and environmental chemicals.

In this connection, particular attention was directed towards pollution by harmful substances, their residues and impurities, since foods belong to those media with which man is in closest contact and through which he is involved in the cycle of substances ("food web").

Despite all efforts undertaken for more than 10 years it has become increasingly apparent in Federal Germany that the important political task of "recognition, assessment and diminishment of health hazards for man and animal" is in the citizen's opinion more and more closely related to chemical substances. So, a study made by a German polling institute (Allensbach) revealed that for 47 per cent - and, hence, most of the citizens of Federal Germany who were polled - "poisoned" foods ranked first. This concern still ranks above the fear of war, or of nuclear weapons or of a potential road accident. Similar results were obtained in a poll carried out by the EEC Commission in 1982, according to which 77 per cent of the citizens of Federal Germany were more concerned about environment than about any other of the many problems nowadays facing us[1].

Since 1974 environmental problems have prompted the establishment of a number of important institutions in Federal Germany. Among these are

- the establishment of the Centre of Detection and Assessment of Environmental Chemicals, belonging to the Federal Public Health Office in Berlin
- the foundation of the Environmental Federal Office in Berlin and
- the setting up of a senatorial commission concerned with the control of resides in foods, attached to the German Research Society. Since 1973 this commission has regularly held scientific colloquia on residues in milk and milk products, meat, poultry, human milk, cereals, fish and other substrates and has provided assistance to the government, giving it some practice in taking basic decisions by means of their communications.

Since in Federal Germany all scientific effort has failed so far to promote the feeling among the population that the problems relating to chemicals in our environment are under control from the scientific and the practical point of view, an attempt has been made in the following paper to discuss the ideas and reactions of the consumer in connection with the environmental legislation concerning agriculture.

---

[1] KOCH, E.R., VAHRENHOLT, F. Situation of the nation. Environmental atlas of the Federal Republic of Germany. Geo-Verlag Gruner & Jahr, Hamburg, 1983.

Fields of agricultural environment protection of direct influence on the consumer

A distinction must be made between seven major fields of environmental protection which are of importance to agriculture and, hence, also to the consumer:

- ecology
- nature protection and preservation of the countryside
- air pollution
- noise
- waste management
- water economy
- environmental chemicals and drugs

Ecology is the science of the interrelationships or interactions in the environment. In natural ecosystems there exist cycles which characterise each ecosystem. The main basic elements of an ecosystem are the producers which bring out energy-rich substances via nutrients and solar energy. The consumers ingest and transform the substances made available by the producers. The material formed by producers which are dying off and by consumers is transformed by a third group, the decomposers, into simple mineral nutrients.

Natural systems are capable of self-regulation and are characterised by the fact that their production of substances and nutrition of their organisms are associated with low residue formation and strains.

Important ecological approaches within the framework of environmental politics in Federal Germany are, for instance, the

- Law on Aircraft Noise
- Petrol-lead Law
- Detergent Law
- Law on Emission Control
- Law on Waste Disposal
- Law on Water Regime
- Law on Nature Protection
- Law on Environmental Chemicals

In the field of <u>nature protection and preservation of the</u>
<u>countryside</u> steady expansion of production and consumption in the last
few decades has led to a continuing loss of the countryside in Federal
Germany. From 1968 to 1978 the agricultural areas decreased by 3.4 per
cent, wasteland environs by 8.8 per cent and the uncultivated moorland
by 16.1 per cent, whilst during the same period of time the space
required for traffic, industrial areas, etc., increased by 15 per cent.
One of the immediate consequences of this consumption of the countryside
is that the existence of up to two-thirds of the plant and animal
species is threatened. Only about 20 per cent of the Federal Territory
still consists of uninterrupted living spaces with low traffic density.

Beside water and foods, <u>air</u> is our most important "food". One of
the major sources of air pollution is the industrial and power economy.
The most important and most frequent air pollutants are

- carbon monoxide
- sulphur dioxide (SO_2)
- nitric oxides (NOx)
- fluorine and heavy metal compounds
- dust
- strongly smelling substances

The consequences of air pollution are serious and may not only lead
to an impairment and affecting of human health, but also to damage to
the health of animals, to vegetation, and so on. In Federal Germany the
main basis of the prevention of air pollution is the Federal Law on
Emission Control, which was passed in 1974 with the corresponding
regulations and the Technical Instruction (Technische Anleitung) for the
Prevention of Air Pollution (TA Air). For agriculture this field of
environmental protection is of comparatively minor importance.

In the same way a connection can only be established to a very
limited extent between <u>noise</u> in the field of environment protection and
agriculture.

In Federal Germany 500 million tonnes of <u>waste</u> are produced annually. Agricultural waste accounts for 260 million tonnes, the greatest part being utilised as fertiliser or feeding stuff. The legal basis of waste disposal is the Waste Disposal Law from 1972. In the agricultural field problems associated with waste are mainly of importance in connection with intensive livestock keeping. This applies to pig and poultry management. Problems associated with cattle keeping arise only in individual cases.

With increasing industrialisation and population density <u>water</u> consumption is rising in Federal Germany. Currently each inhabitant is estimated to use an average of 142 litres of water per day. The legal basis of water protection in Federal Germany is the Water Regime Law from 1976. In addition, mention should be made of the law regarding the waste water tax (1978) and the Detergent Law (1975).

Due to its particular importance to the consumer the field on <u>environmental chemicals and drugs</u> is discussed later under a separate heading.

<u>Which of the legal activities of the Federal Government are of particular importance to the consumer?</u>

From the environmental viewpoint the following legislation is of importance to both agriculture and the consumer:

- <u>Regulation regarding plant protection</u>
    - Law on Protection of Plants

- <u>Food Regulations</u>
    - Law on Foodstuffs and Commodities (August 15, 1974)
    - Ordinance regarding Tolerance Limits for Pesticides
    - DDT Ordinance
    - Mercury Ordinance (fish)
    - Drinking Water Ordinance
    - Aflatoxin Ordinance
    - Ordinance regarding Substances with Pharmacological Effect

- Feed Regulation
  - Feed Law (July 2, 1975)

- Drug Regulation
  - Drug Law (August 24, 1976 and February 24, 1983)

- Meat Inspection Regulation
  - Law on Meat Inspection (October 29, 1940 and September 2, 1975)

- Water Regulation
  - Law on Water Regime
  - Law on Waste Water Tax

- Regulation regarding Emission Control
  - Federal Law on Emission Control (March 15, 1974)
  - Technical Instruction for the Prevention of Air Pollution
  - Ordinance regarding Big Combustion Plants

- Waste Disposal Regulation
  - Law on Waste Disposal (June 7, 1972 and January 5, 1977)

- Regulation regarding Removal of Animal Bodies
  - Law on Removal of Animal Bodies (September 2, 1975)

- Nature Protection Regulation
  - Law on Nature Protection (December 20, 1976)
  - Law on the Washington Convention regarding Species Protection

Since the consumer in Federal Germany is, regarding legislation, particularly interested in problems associated with residues and contaminants in foods of animal origin, these will be discussed later in more detail.

Which of the residues and contaminants in foods of animal origin are of particular interest to the consumer?

In meat and meat products, eggs and poultry and in fish too, a great number of residues and contaminants can occur. The following survey shows the main groups of substances:

Residues and contaminants in foods of animal origin

1. **Drugs for animals**
   Antibiotics; formulations for parasite control; hormones and substances of hormonal, anabolic effects; psychopharmacological drugs and beta-blocker; teat disinfectants.

2. **Pesticides**
   Insecticides, fungicides, herbicides.

3. **Polychlorinated biphenyls (PCB)**

4. **Contaminants occurring during production, treatment and processing**
   Nitrate, nitrite, nitrosamines; polycyclic aromatic hydrocarbons; detergents and disinfectants; migrating substances

5. **Heavy metals and radionuclides**

6. **Mycotoxins**

   Using milk and milk products as an example, Table 1 (below) demonstrates how milk and milk products can be contaminated by residues of rather different origin.

Table 1. <u>Milk and milk products with residues of chemicals</u>
<u>of different origin</u>

ARABLE FARMING AND ENVIRONMENT

FARM ANIMAL	Agrochemicals	MILKING AND PROCESSING
<u>Veterinary Drugs</u>	e.g. Pesticides, Stock Protection Growth Promotors/Inhibitors	<u>Hygiene Formula-tions</u>
e.g. Antibiotics Antiparasiticides Neuroleptics	<u>Emissions</u> e.g. Aerosols, Fumes, Dusts	e.g. Cleaning and Disinfecting Agents Insecticides
<u>Feed Additives</u>	<u>Minerals of the Soil</u>	<u>Surfaces</u>
e.g. Trace Elements Feed Drugs	e.g. Lead <u>Environmental Organics</u> e.g. Mycotoxins, PAHs PCBs	e.g. Metals (PB,Sn,Zn,Ca) Vulcanisers Plasticisers Stabilisers PCBs
	<u>Radionuclides</u>	<u>Microbial Products</u> e.g. Mycotoxins

<u>Milk and Milk Products</u>
with
<u>Secretory and/or Postsecretory</u>
<u>Residues of Chemicals of</u>
<u>Different Origin</u>

Among the chemical substances occurring in foods not only residues and contaminants should be mentioned, but also the so-called additives which are, however, left out of consideration here.

What regulations protect the consumer from drug residues?

The use of drugs is indispensable in modern animal production, their application serving not only the purpose of treating diseases that have already occurred, but, in many cases, where preventive measures are necessary. The broad field of parasite control in farm animals should be mentioned here, among others.

In Federal Germany both the Food and the Drug Laws include provisions ensuring that drugs do not occur in food as residues.

According to Section 15 of the Food Law it is prohibited to put foods of animal origin into circulation, when substances exhibiting a pharmacological effect or their conversion (metabolic) products have been found in or on them. If substances with pharmacological effects which are either registered or approved as drugs are applied to the living animal, foods obtained from the animal are not allowed to be put into circulation, unless the withholding period established when registering or approving the drug has been observed. If no specific withdrawal periods are established for the individual drug, foods are allowed to be put into circulation 5 days at the earliest after application of these drugs. To protect the consumer the Federal Government is authorised to establish maximum levels for substances with pharmacological effect which can still be accepted in or on foods. Further, defined substances with pharmacological effects can be completely or partially (for defined purposes) excluded from application to the animal or can even be prohibited altogether.

According to the Drug Law drugs are on principle subjected to approval (formerly; to registration). The documents to be submitted for approval must be submitted by the producer and contain detailed information on potentially occurring residues in foods. Decision on approval is taken by the Federal Health Office in Berlin. When approving a drug for a defined field of application withholding periods must be established. Approval of drugs can be revoked or repealed. Drugs which contain defined substances or preparations must not be sold without prescription. For all drugs containing substances whose effects are not generally known a doctor's prescription is automatically required. These drugs must not be sold to the consumer without a veterinary surgeon's prescription. With very few exceptions distribution of drugs via the itinerant trade is prohibited. When approving a drug an analytical procedure has, in each case, to be indicated which is applicable in practice and sensitive enough to allow control and monitoring of withholding periods.

Summing up, it can, therefore, be stated that residues of drugs in foods of animal origin are not likely to present problems in Federal Germany, if the legislation in force is observed. In practice, however, it must be said that the clear-cut legal regulations are not always observed. It is, for instance, known that

- control of the presence of drug residues is, to some extent, inadequately carried out
- application of prohibited or non-approved drugs cannot be eliminated, and
- certain drugs are used in cases which are not included in the officially approved list (e.g. hormones as fattening aid).

How is the consumer protected from pesticide residues?

The Food Law in force in Federal Germany has two aims:

1. Protection of the consumer from health risks and
2. Protection of the consumer from deception.

To safeguard the consumer's health, the production or treatment of foods in such a manner that their consumption may lead to health risks is prohibited. For this basic provision there exist extensive warranties for the protection of health or for issuance of hygiene ordinances (Sections 8-10 of the Food Law). Foods containing pesticides or similar substances must not be put into circulation unless tolerance limits are kept for the individual pesticides. An extensive regulation concerning tolerance limits (for foods of both animal and plant origin) includes a few hundred substances which must not be present in defined foods above defined tolerance limits. Substances which are not included in this regulation must not be present in foods. The somewhat problematic nature of this regulation concerning pesticide tolerance limits lies in the fact that defined foods may be "mixed" in order to guarantee that the final product contains residue levels below the legal tolerance limit.

According to the Law on Plant Protection pesticides must not be imported or professionally distributed in Federal Germany unless they are approved by the Federal Biological Centre of Agriculture and Forestry. Approval includes a special procedure which presupposes thorough examination of numerous documents. Approval granted for a pesticide expires after a period of 10 years. It can be renewed or fixed for a shorter period of time. Persons using pesticides professionally must inform the competent authority accordingly prior to the beginning of their activity. Approval of a pesticide involves detailed indications on its fields of application and the withholding periods which must be observed.

Summing up, it can, hence, be stated that the Food Law and the legislation regarding pesticides including numerous regulations guarantee on principle that harmful levels of pesticide residues must not occur in foods of plant and animal origin. But here too implementation of the regulations is somewhat problematic, in that it is almost impossible to control the extensive catalogue of active substances included in, for example, the regulation concerning maximum pesticide levels, covering as it does such a diversity of foods of plant and animal origin. There exist, for instance, far more than 30 individual regulations for milk alone, and, as regards foods of plant origin, far more than 200 individual substances are listed for which varying tolerance limits are established for widely varying foods.

Feed Law and residues in food

The Feed Law in Federal Germany aims to promote animal production in such a manner that

- the efficiency of the livestock is maintained and improved and
- the products obtained from the livestock meet the requirements in terms of quality and legislation.

Further, the animal's health shall not be impaired by feed, and
deception must be prevented when dealing with feed, additives and pre-
mixes. In the EEC countries the important regulations concerning feed
additives and harmful substances in feeds are, to a large extent,
uniformly regulated by guidelines which have been integrated into
national law. Research into the carry over of such substances has
gained particular importance recently, since defined undesirable
substances present in feeds or harmful substances may pass into foods
and cause problems, in particular, when large amounts of the feeding
stuffs concerned are given.

In certain regions of Federal Germany feeding of imported feed has
markedly increased in the last 20 years. Whilst in 1960 only about
300 kg of imported feeds were annually fed per cow in various regions of
North Germany, the quantities indicated for 1982/83 amounted to
2000-3000 kg/cow a year. If we consider the markedly varying feeding
techniques, it becomes apparent that the efficiency of regulations
concerning tolerance limits in feeds can only be limited, since the
carry over of undesirable substances is dependent on the total amount of
the substances ingested. If markedly varying rations with different
concentrations of individual components are fed, established tolerance
limits may be sufficient in one case and completely inadequate in
another case.

From extensive studies it is known in Federal Germany from which
parts of the world raw materials for feeding stuffs with particularly
high amounts of harmful substances are imported. Here, for instance,
attention has to be drawn to aflatoxin contamination of peanut, cotton
seed and cocoa products. This applies also to HCH contamination of
ricebran from certain East Asian countries. In view of these facts the
Feed Law in Federal Germany provides not only regulations concerning
composite and single feeds, but also special regulations concerning
certain raw materials containing levels of harmful substances above
defined tolerance limits (e.g. max. aflatoxin levels in raw materials of
0.2 mg/kg).

Summing up, it can be stated that the Feed Law in Federal Germany is an effective means of controlling contamination of food originating from animals. With increasing feeding of imported concentrates the requirements concerning maximum levels of undesirable substances are constantly being tightened up. Systematic control is also of decisive importance for the efficiency of this procedure. This applies, in particular, to feeding stuffs from countries where pesticides, etc., are used which are not approved in Federal Germany. As in the fields of the Food and the Drug Laws, control measures also need to be extended in respect of the Feed Law.

Are additives in foods a reason for discussion?

In Federal Germany the principle of prohibition as regards the use of additives (Section 11 Food Law) has been established. On principle, therefore, such additives to foods which are not approved by the Federal Health Office in Berlin are prohibited. Only a few harmless substances such as defined enzymes and cultures of micro-organisms are not subjected to prohibition which is generally applicable to the use of additives.

In extensive regulations those additives are stated for the individual foods which may be present in these foods up to a certain tolerance level. For defined foods (e.g. milk) additives must not be used. The additives themselves are subjected to detailed analytical control. The quality of the additives is clearly defined in terms of their purity and toleration of potential impurities or secondary ingredients.

In Federal Germany there are special regulations on so-called dietary foods in the Diet Ordinance. Finally, there is also a clause stating that most additives used must be named (dyestuffs, preservatives, antioxidants, etc.). Hence it can be stated that although the problems associated with additives in Federal Germany are frequently discussed in connection with "chemicalisation" of foods, there are no indications that health hazards exist. The consumer tolerates the use of additives to a considerable extent.

How does the consumer react to the discussion on residues,
contaminants and additives in foods?

In Federal Germany numerous consumers, in particular the younger
people, have the desire for "healthy food". From the viewpoint of
physiology of nutrition, however, no clear-cut definition of "healthy"
foods exists. This wording actually originates from the colloquial
speech of certain groups of consumers for which "healthy foods" are
often "other", that is to say, alternative foods. Many citizens of
Federal Germany classify foods as being "healthy" from the following
viewpoints

- reduction of calories
- high nutrient contents
- without added chemicals
- minor industrial treatment

There are currently about 250 so-called "bio-shops" in Federal
Germany, although this number fluctuates considerably. In addition,
there are about 1700 health shops and about 1000 sales sections in
pharmacies and chemist's shops which offer "alternative" foods. Little
is known on the figures for sales volume. The health shops' turnover
totalled more than 800 million DM in 1982. Most of the bio-shops are in
the cities and only few of them in rural areas. The bio-shops have
about 60 customers on an average per day, each spending between 10 and
20 DM. Annual sales of 150,000 DM per bio-shop or a total of
40 million DM can be estimated. This is less than 0.4 °/oo of the total
volume of food sales of the retail trade.

However, the desire of the population in Federal Germany for
"healthy foods" is not solely characterised by the turnover of health
shops and bio-shops. If foods with a "healthy" image are considered,
there has been a considerable increase in sales. Turnover and
production of special cereals, such as oat flakes, muesli, corn flakes,
vegetable juice and low-calorie refreshing drinks considerably increased
in the period from 1970-1980. Turnover of dietary food increased from
1500 million DM to 2200 million DM between 1970-1975. Similar rates of
increase have been established for other products.

The volume of "alternative" production of "healthy foods" is negligible in Federal Germany. There are probably about 700 farms producing "alternative" foods. They account for no more than 12,500-20,000 ha of the farmland or 0.1-0.2 per cent of the total farmland in Federal Germany. Moreover, due to the analytical results there are justifiable doubts whether all of the "healthy foods" offered are actually as good as they promise.

The following Table shows particulars on the products which are obtained in health shops and bio-shops:

Table 2. Particulars on the products obtained in health shops and bio-shops
(several answers were possible, particulars in %)

	bio-shops	health shops
Cereals, meal	80	
Muesli, Muesli ingredients	50	60*
Nuts, dried fruits	40	30
Spices, herbs	34	50
Honey, jam	32	**
Drinks	30	49
Fresh fruit and vegetable	28	22
Pulse	20	6
Oil, margarine	19	59
Milk, milk products	14	41
Books, journals	27	
Other "non-food" articles	21	35*
Dietary foods	**	18
Drugs free on sale	**	27

* different answering categories on questionnaires for health shop customers
** answering category was not included in the questionnaire concerned

The details on the reasons for choosing the diet observed by the customers of health shops and bio-shops are given below:

Table 3. Indications of the customers of health shops and bio-shops on their diet

Observance of a defined diet	Bio-shops	Health shops
	(proportion in %)	
Strict observance	27	22
Observance, but not strict	43	41
No particular diet	30	37

Those who indicated they observed a defined diet gave the following particulars:

Highly nutritious cost	38	45
Lacto(ovo) vegetarian	23	14
Strict vegetarian	7	6
Anthroposophic	8	4
Macrobiotic	13	1
Reducing diet	–	8
Diet ordered by the doctor	2	16

Monetary aspects

Production of foods with low or without residue contents is undoubtedly more expensive than that involving the use of active substances such as pesticides or drugs for animals. In Federal Germany the prices of the so-called alternative foods are estimated to be up to twice as high as "normal" foods.

It is apparent that in Federal Germany only a comparatively small group of consumers is ready to meet the higher expenses incurred in connection with "biological" foods. The total volume of food sales in bio-shops and health shops accounts for only a small percentage of the total volume of food sold by the retail trade.

To safeguard foods with low or without residue contents, intensification of the control measures in connection with the Food Law, the Drug Law and the Feed Law is an important aspect. The expenditure potentially required in this context is considerable, for corresponding preconditions in terms of staff and instruments must be provided in monitoring itself and in the research institutions. In Federal Germany the States are responsible for food control. In veterinary and chemical research institutes, approximately 500,000 samples are examined annually. The number of samples is dependent on the respective population figure of the States of the Federal Republic. As regards the kind of samples, the distinction must be made between the so-called random samples and the suspicious samples. From the ratio of these samples the number of potential objections and also the expenditure associated with these objections can be derived.

It is hardly possible to make a quantitative estimate of any intensification of the control of foods, drugs and feeds. However, it may be assumed that the costs incurred by an analysis for residues and contaminants (which is more difficult to carry out) are within the range between 100 and 200 DM.

If the number of examinations were increased annually by only 10,000 and the costs for a more difficult analysis amounted to about 100 DM, this alone would annually cause additional costs of the order of 1 million DM.

THE EFFECTS OF AN IMPLEMENTATION OF STRICTER LEGISLATION:
THE REACTION OF THE CONSUMER

Emeritus Professor G.P. Wibberley
Wye College (University of London)

I am a retired Professor of Countryside Planning. This subject is
a wide one because it deals with the problems of rural land resources
and with the rural activities that take place on them, whether these
activities come from within the rural economy or are generated outside
but take place in rural areas. From this background and with hindsight
of the earlier lectures it might have been better if the format of this
seminar had been changed. It could have structured in reverse. We
should perhaps have started by listing what society in general appears
to want rather than talking about what agriculturalists would like
consumers to want. This appears to be a dangerous tendency in
agricultural circles in Britain. I would therefore have liked us to
discuss consumer needs and aspirations first, then looked at the 'de
jure' and 'de facto' positions on environmental legislation and ended by
discussing the cost both to the farmer and to society in general.

I have also noticed with interest and some concern that there have
been very few comments in this group as to the range of attitudes and
policies in different political groups and parties on this matter of
environmental restraints on farmers. The different political groups are
beginning to look at this matter in different ways. We have, as our
German friends will know, in this country at the moment, a Tory
government. (The word "Tory" seems to mean a very conservative kind of
Conversative.) This group is strongly influenced by land-owning and
farming interests, particularly in the Cabinet. The Tory group, on the
whole, believes in voluntary arrangements for very many things, with a
minimum of environmental restraints on farming practice and the full
recoupment in financial terms of any such restraints if farming incomes
are likely to be reduced.

Perhaps our German friends do not realise that in our Parliament there is the general principle that if a person has a pecuniary interest in the matter under discussion, then they should so declare it. It so happens, and this has been accepted for generations, that the one pecuniary interest you do not have to declare if you are discussing a subject in the House of Commons or the House of Lords is land ownership. This surprising omission is responsible for some of the curious things that happen. For example, the Wildlife and Countryside Act, which has been mentioned by many British colleagues here, went through long discussions throughout 1980/81. If one reads the Hansard reports of exactly what was said, it is clear that the amendments put forward were often very well argued and convincing, and any reader would have said that these amendments should have been accepted. But a review of the voting picture suggests that a large number of land-owning peers had obviously come up to London on the particular days and automatically voted against the suggestion of a restraint on land-owning or farming practice.

Now, in contrast, there is another party in Britain at the moment, known as the Labour Party, which has a very different set of policies. They would bring in more environmental restraints, particularly those related to landscape maintenance and to wildlife protection and they would bring in restraints relating to the protection of the rights of animals to lead a more natural type of existence.

Thus during our own discussion here we ought to think about various political attitudes and policies in relation to environmental matters and not assume that we can discuss and settle many of these controversial matters as if political parties did not exist and as if there are no major differences between them. I do not know if this is the case in Germany, but we have this curious belief in Britain that every rural problem can be settled if enough rural people of goodwill are brought together as somehow or other an agreed solution will emerge from such a group. In practice, however, the British countryside is riven with factions, not only political, but between the elite and the under-privileged in relation to geographical area, possessions and access to physical and social services.

In my opinion the concern for improved rural environments for human beings will probably become more strongly linked in the future with more humane and outdoor treatment of animals kept for food. The environmental and the animal welfare lobbies will come closer together, and if they combine and can agree on policies they will be very powerful. I sense in Germany that you are more sensitive in this area than we British. But if this combination of interests were to happen in this country it would mean that the two million people who are now active members of environmental interest groups would be joined with the one million members who are concerned and active in animal welfare groups, making a total of three million people which is a considerable force for change.

At this point may I put before you a list of what appears to be the environmental aspirations of the general citizen in this country. I have thought about this a certain amount to see if I could put down in words what people in environmental groups and in other groups seem to want when one talks to them and examines their literature. The general citizen appears to want a countryside of considerable variety, with mixed land uses and tree and plant colour; a patchwork, a mosaic of uses and colours, with considerable neatness and open sweeps of cultivated land and yet wildness in certain places. I think there is a great wish for this sort of countryside amongst young as well as the old. Not very long ago I was adjudicating at the London School of Economics on plans for the British countryside in the year 2000 and from the students I heard quite conservative comments as to what they wanted; very much along the lines I have indicated. They felt there should be a wide range of ecological habitats, with a rich variety of flora and fauna.

There seems to be a general wish for a wide range of farm sizes, with farm buildings in local styles and building materials or with harmonious additions to them. There is certainly agreement that farm practices that pollute should be subject to control and to penalties.

I sense that there are a large group of people who are becoming more and more convinced that planning controls must come into the countryside. They have been present in urban areas for a long time.

These planning controls should cover only major farming changes, for example, to farmhouses and buildings and major changes thereof, on woodland, on important trees and old important hedges, and over important nature conservation areas so that they are not scrubbed out for all time.

There is also growing concern about intensive livestock practices. Again it is interesting that our German colleagues have appeared to be much more sensitive in this area, whereas the British generally and British members of agricultural organisations still show an insensitivity in this area which surprises and saddens me. But there are millions of people who feel that it is right and proper that the animals we use for food should be allowed reasonable natural movements and that they should, as much as possible, have some experience of outdoor life. I know it is fashionable to decry the extremist animal rights' movements, but there is a general feeling that we have gone much too far in our insensitivity to animal cruelty. Certainly as a farming person, I am aware that cruelty to animals has always been present in farming practice, but I am shocked to my bones that, as the decades have passed, an insensitivity to animal welfare has crept into British farming practice. I suspect that human societies that are cruel to animals can also be cruel and insensitive to their fellow human beings.

Lastly, there is a growing concern that farmers should pay their fair share of local and national taxes, and that they should be subject to similar laws and regulations experienced by their fellow citizens. There is concern, particularly in Britain, that we have made an over privileged group of our farming compatriots and that steps should be taken to bring farmers and land owners back to the status of ordinary citizens.

I would like to suggest that there are a large number of people who would accept the general picture I have drawn. Certainly the three million people in environmental interest groups and animal welfare groups accept it and they are actively working for this sort of countryside at the present time. For evidence we can look at opinion polls that are available on such matters in the EEC, in the United States and in Britain. There was a 1983 EEC opinion survey which covered 10 thousand people. The results showed that something under 10 per cent of these people expressed no concern at all on environmental matters; that 55 per cent of them, interestingly enough, did not feel much concern about their everyday local environment, but were concerned about large, non-local environmental matters, for example, threats to sea life and beaches from oil spillages, disposal of chemical, industrial and nuclear waste, the growing scourge of acid rain and concern about large scale de-forestation. It is as if there are a large number of people ready to be mobilised and ready to provide funds for large scale problems concerned with the environment in which their interest has been aroused. The World Wildlife Fund capitalises very much on this type of interest. Sixty per cent of the sample chose to protect the environment even if the measures taken made individuals spend more money through higher prices. And a similar proportion agreed with environmental controls even if it meant restricting economic growth. Similar results were found in earlier polls of 1973, 1976 and 1978, and they have been also shown in polls of this kind taken in the United States.

Let us now look at the British opinion polls. In 1980-82 it was found that 64 per cent of a balanced sample favoured raising taxes to control pollution, but the majority were against this if it meant the loss of jobs. But in 1983 there was a Mori poll. Now our German colleagues may not know about the Mori polls in this country. Mori is a firm which specialises in opinion polls and it has built up an enviable reputation for being right. As a result, it wields considerable influence, and so the Countryside Commission decided recently to use this organisation to see how British people felt about the environment.

1991 people were interviewed. Of these, 53 per cent said they would support an increase in income tax of a penny in the pound to pay for protection of wildlife and the general environment. 26 per cent said they would oppose such a move and 31 per cent of the sample had donated money to a conservation charity in the previous year and 4 per cent claimed to be a member of a conservation society. The Countryside Commission has blazoned those figures abroad and feels very proud of the results; certainly the conservation movement generally has reported them and I sense that politicians were really impressed by the results.

We know a lot about environmental groups in Britain now because a
colleague of mine, Philip Lowe, who was lecturer in Countryside Planning
when I was a Professor at University College London, has, with his
research assistant, produced an interesting book called, "Environmental
Interest Groups in Politics" (Lowe and Goyder, 1983), Allen and Unwin.
This records for the first time the growth and the nature and influence
of environmental interest groups. They are roughly about two million
people in active membership; in 1980 they had a total finance of £26
million in subscriptions, which went from just a few pounds up to £12
per person per year. This £26 million is more than the British
Government spends each year on the Nature Conservancy Council, the
Countryside Commission and the Historic Buildings Commission. The links
of these environmental interest groups with government departments are
very selective and I think you will find that book valuable if you want
to see how this curious link between voluntary and official groups works
in this country.

The authors point out that the Ministry of Agriculture in this
country only supports one environmental interest group with money and
active help. This is the Farming and Wildlife Advisory Groups (FWAG).
It does not support any others. On the other hand, the Department of
the Environment and the Nature Conservancy Council cooperate both
financially and otherwise with a much wider range of environmental
interest groups.

In the United Kingdom, on average, five people out of every
thousand belong to these environmental interest groups and it is up to
between ten and twenty per thousand in Kent, Sussex, Devon,
Northumberland, and Cumbria. In other words the interest is quite
spotty.

May I end with a comment which may be thought controversial. If,
for example, farmers in Great Britain paid their fair share of local
taxes (or what we call rates), which were taken off the shoulders of
farmers during the 1930's because of the agricultural depression of that
time, but which, a Royal Commission has argued, should be now

re-introduced - if, as I say, local rates on farms were reintroduced, this would produce about £150 million a year, a sum sufficient to pay for the cost of extending the statutory planning system so that it covered the types of environmental control of agricultural land use and practice which I have suggested previously and for which there is growing support.

Produced by Greyhound Lithographic Studio, Wye, Ashford, Kent